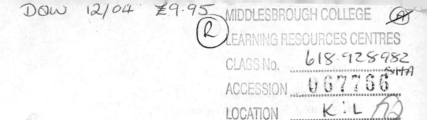

I'm Not Naughty – I'm Autistic

Middlesbrough College

Roman Road

Middlesbrough

TS5 5PJ

D0177273

of related interest

The Dragons of Autism
Autism as a Source of Wisdom
Olga Holland
ISBN 1 84310 741 4

Freaks, Geeks and Asperger Syndrome
A User Guide to Adolescence
Luke Jackson
ISBN 1 84310 098 3

Through the Eyes of Aliens
A Book about Autistic People
Jasmine Lee O'Neill
ISBN 1 85302 710 3

Growing Up Severely Autistic
They Call Me Gabriel
Kate Rankin
ISBN 1 85302 891 6

Dangerous Encounters – Avoiding Perilous
Situations with Autism
A Streetwise Guide for all Emergency Responders,
Retailers and Parents
Bill Davis and Wendy Goldband Schunick
ISBN 1 84310 732 5

I'm Not Naughty – I'm Autistic

Jodi's Journey

Jean Shaw

Jessica Kingsley Publishers
London and Philadelphia

First published in the United Kingdom in 2002
by Jessica Kingsley Publishers
116 Pentonville Road
London N1 9JB, UK
and
400 Market Street, Suite 400
Philadelphia, PA 19106, USA

www.jkp.com

Copyright © Jean Shaw 2002
Second impression 2003
Third impression 2004
Fourth impression 2005

Library of Congress Cataloging in Publication Data
Shaw, Jean (Jean Kathleen), 1955-
I'm not naughty--I'm autistic / Jean Shaw.
p. cm.
ISBN 1-84310-105-X (pbk. : alk. Paper)
1. Shaw, Jodi, --Mental health. 2. Autism--Patients--Biography. 3. Autistic children--Biography. 4. Autistic children--Family relationships. 5. Parents of autistic children. I. Title.
RJ506.A9 S525 2002
618.92'8982'0092--dc21
[B]

2002070925

British Library Cataloguing in Publication Data
A CIP catalogue record for this book is available from the British Library

ISBN-13: 978 1 84310 105 5
ISBN-10: 1 84310 105 X

Printed and Bound in Great Britain by
Athenaeum Press, Gateshead, Tyne and Wear

*With special thanks to my family
and particularly my parents
whose love, understanding and
acceptance have helped me
through the difficult times.*

I'm sure in the great scheme of things
As part of the Master Plan
Each one has a role to play
To help his fellow man.

I don't know what my role is
What I'm supposed to do
But now I'm half-way through my life
Perhaps this is a clue?

Foreword

Jodi's Journey is written for no one in particular and everyone in general. It is the story of his life so far, interspersed with some of the little facets of autism. The writer hopes it will give a small insight into this invisible, inexplicable and, thus far, apparently incurable disability.

Autistic – who me?

I am Jodi's mother and have written the story as though he is the narrator. Jodi does not use language. He says words and that is not the same thing. There are situations in this story therefore when I can only presume to know what he was thinking or why he did something. Only one person knows for certain and he is not disclosing that information – yet!

Jodi's Journey

Here goes – my journey written by my secretary. Mums do have their uses. I'm not sure how this works. I've never attempted this before so if I go off at a tangent don't worry – it's one of the quirks of autism. We don't think in the way you so-called 'normal' people do.

I suppose I ought to introduce myself at this point, so, hello my name is Jodi Shaw. I'm twelve years old, almost thirteen, and apparently I'm hormonal. Life history – well, my mum had a normal pregnancy and my birth was regular. I developed as babies do and reached all the landmarks at the appropriate times. Actually that's not quite true as I was quite advanced with crawling and walking. I obviously felt the need to catch up with my older brother who, with a twenty-one-month head start on me, seemed to be having much more fun. Another thing I was advanced at was cutting my teeth because at the age of five months my mother decided it was getting too dangerous to breastfeed so I hit the bottle. Boy, did I hit the bottle, but I also indulged in all those other deliciously appetizing meals babies get served up. I thrived on them, at least the amount I managed to get in my mouth instead of on my hands and face. I used to grab the spoon and try to help. I just wasn't very good at it – too impatient or was that greedy? Anyway, I even ate up all my fruit and vegetables. What a good boy! Yes, life was ideal when I was a baby.

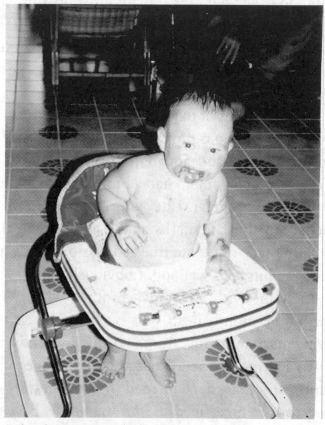

What do you mean, 'It's all gone'?

Everything went well until I was ten months old and had a febrile convulsion. We lived in Brunei at the time where it is pretty hot. Anyway, I managed to catch some sort of virus and got a temperature. My mum did her best to cool me down – you know the sort of thing, Calpol, tepid baths, wet flannels, clothes off, lying in an air-conditioned room under a ceiling fan but my temperature shot up to 104 degrees and I had a fit. Apparently I went blue and she thought I'd died. We dashed off to the doctor who sent for an ambulance. By this time I had recovered and was fine. It was all exciting stuff though and I was getting lots of attention. It was great.

I had a bit of a relapse in the hospital and had another febrile convulsion whilst the doctor was examining me but apparently that was normal too. They said lots of children get them and tend to grow out of them by the age of about five. If I'd played my cards right I could have had lots of attention over the next four years but at ten months I hadn't much experience of cards. I'd suffered no ill effects from the episode and for a while I was fine.

Things went back to normal. I ate, I drank, I played, I slept and I enjoyed being with people, but then the pack of cards must have changed and I was dealt a bad hand. It got me attention all right but in a totally different way. I became autistic. Sounds glamorous but it isn't. Apparently it is one of the worst mental disabilities to deal with because there is no cure, and as no two autists are the same, there is no prognosis. That's tough.

Autism changed everything. My mum said I was fine until I had the measles, mumps, rubella (MMR) injection. This was a relatively new vaccine but my brother had had his and had been okay. Opinion is growing that it should not be given to any child who is obviously unwell at the time, had allergies or reactions to previous vaccinations, or had a history of fits. Whilst the government's line on this is that it is in the child's best interest to accept the MMR, an increasing number of parents and doctors are beginning to question whether it is a step too far in the sense that it is a combination of vaccines against diseases which children could not catch together naturally all at once. The triple vaccine may well be fine for the majority of children, but for those susceptible to things like febrile convulsions or bowel problems the effects of the triple MMR jab are not clear.

Anyway, when I had my injection, which had only been introduced two years previously, the possible adverse side effects were never in question. As my febrile convulsions were on our medical records there was no reason to suppose it would cause a problem. None of the previous injections had caused anything in me other than a red mark on my arm and at the time of the MMR I was perfectly healthy. Okay, perhaps I shouldn't gripe – at least I won't get measles, mumps or rubella, but which would you rather have? That's a stupid question really. You can't possibly imagine what it's like to be autistic just as anyone who has sight or hearing can't realistically imagine what it must be like to be blind or deaf.

Anyway, I changed from being an alert, talkative, happy, interested, lively, loving little bundle who would eat and drink anything into the toddler from hell – and all in the space of a very short period of time. I became thoroughly miserable, completely withdrawn and wouldn't let anyone near me except my mother to whom I clung like a limpet. I needed my space and would walk out of a room when someone entered or cower in a corner. I wouldn't look at anyone, stopped speaking, wouldn't point, couldn't bear to be held or touched, banged my head on the floors and walls and refused to eat anything other than Hula Hoops. (At least I was easy to feed.)

I stopped looking at books or playing with toys. All I did was line them up in very straight lines and I used anything that remotely resembled a stick to bang with. I also posted things. The video machine and the grill for the heating system were favourites, but I also had a tendency to post incoming mail back outside and often Mum would find her letters lying on the outside doormat. It was fine for the bills but not the ones she actually wanted to receive. I lost concentration and never sat still. If I wasn't climbing on something I was jumping on it. My pièce de résistance though was a high-pitched squeal which went through everyone. Not such a good boy!

Needless to say it became obvious to everyone there was something wrong with me. Many theories were expounded. We had just moved to the UK from Brunei and it was a complete change. We were only intending to stay in the UK for three months so were lodging with my grandparents. The weather was different, the people were a different colour, houses were much smaller and the whole set-up was confusing. My dad had also disappeared to America to do some flying course and so, apart from my mum and big brother, I was surrounded by people I didn't really know too well. Could it be that I was traumatized?

The next theory was one of teeth. I was cutting my four large molars all at once – no mean feat I can tell you, especially when you are only eighteen months old. I was in a lot of pain and also had lots of ear infections. The doctor gave me loads of antibiotics. What he didn't give me was acidobifidus, or the advice that this should always be taken when you are on antibiotics so that the good bacteria in the body aren't destroyed with the bad bacteria. I know better now.

Things came to a head at Christmas 1990 when I challenged everyone's festive spirit with my dreadful behaviour. Someone banged a sweet tin directly behind me as loud as they could. I think it was an attempt to drown out my squealing but I didn't flinch. Not a muscle twitched or an eyelash flickered. To all intents and purposes I hadn't heard it. 'Good grief – he's deaf.' Suddenly, even my most annoyed family members became sympathetic.

As early as possible in January we sought out the doctor and after examination he said I had glue ear and really enlarged adenoids. He said it was no wonder I was so miserable as I must be in tremendous pain and as I couldn't hear that would explain why I had stopped communicating and screamed endlessly. It never occurred to anyone at the time that it didn't explain why I had also regressed to crawling, stopped playing with my toys, changed my diet, become very antisocial and wouldn't make eye contact or point. Oh well, sort out the worst bits first.

We were told I needed an operation to insert some grommets in the ears which would allow the fluid to drain away and reduce the pressure, but we would have to wait until September to have it done on the NHS. That was nine months away so my parents dug deep and paid for me to have it done in April 1991. It cost £1000, but it's a small price to pay for a happy toddler and the restoration of sanity.

The operation went well. I had the grommets inserted although by the time April arrived the weather had warmed up and the glue had melted so I probably could have done without them anyway.

Unfortunately, I didn't improve. What should have happened was that after the operation when someone came into my room or called my name I should have turned to see what was happening. I didn't. My parents were devastated. It couldn't have been because they'd wasted their money could it? No, it was obviously because now they had to seek other answers to my situation, but from where?

Off we went to the excellent ear, nose and throat (ENT) department at the local hospital, but my mum used to dread taking me there. I was very active and Mum had to wear trainers all the time. They aren't wonderfully glamorous but I was fast and would just disappear where the mood took me. I had no sense of danger, no awareness of other people and no social skills. If I wanted something someone else had, even if it was their personal possession, I would just take it. I wouldn't ask – I couldn't. We never got to see the specialists on time and I wasn't much good at waiting, so Mum lived on the edge whenever we went anywhere. She never knew what I would do. It was no good her explaining to me that you had to share toys with other children because I didn't understand and how could she expect other children to share with me if I wouldn't return the favour. Big problem!

The various hearing tests proved inconclusive, mainly because my attention span was limited to about four seconds. I wouldn't sit still, didn't understand what was expected of me and wouldn't allow anyone close to me, let alone touch me. The result of my nightmarish hospital visits was that the ENT department thought I was probably deaf and issued me with two hearing aids. They instructed my mum to go home and make sure I kept them in. Fat chance!

Postman Pat on the television and the rattling of crisp packets proved to my mum that I had selective hearing. (I'm told that is a trait in men, particularly older married ones.) The hearing aids were discarded and off we headed to see the child psychologist. Now this was an interesting phase which I could tell completely baffled my mum. We had to go into a room and the psychologist would be in there. She wouldn't speak to us though, so we didn't know what we were supposed to do. I think the idea was that she was observing how we interacted with each other. I just did my own thing, seemingly oblivious to my surroundings. I picked up a few toys, lined them up, banged them a bit and climbed on the furniture. Mum tried to talk to me – I ignored her. I appeared unaware of what was going on, but was I? You see, we autists have this special thing called peripheral vision. We can sort of see out of the corner of our eyes so if you really want us to look at something perhaps you should face us in a sideways direction. Clever, eh? I had several sessions with the psychologists and never really understood why I went but after almost two years they gave us their opinion.

Between the ages of three and four and a half my parents were beginning to look older by the second. I was incredibly active, had an improved attention span of at least six seconds and my diet was getting better. I would now eat Hula Hoops, crumpets, digestive biscuits and chicken burgers. Notice they are all round and on the same beige/brown colour spectrum. I didn't need sleep and had about four to five hours broken sleep each night. I rarely slept in the day. Of course, if I was up I needed company – wrong word – supervision. Good old Mum – another use.

That's what autism is pretty much about – using people for our own wants and needs. Still, someone must have told her being a parent isn't easy. Don't get me wrong here, autists aren't deliberately selfish or inconsiderate – it's just the nature of the disability. Oh, and if anyone has any ideas about trying it on with family members to see how much they can get away with – forget it. Autism is a disability – not a disease. It's not contagious so you can't pretend.

A few people in the caring professions got involved and decided I needed help or maybe they took a look at the bags under Mum's eyes and decided she needed some sleep. Initially it came in the form of a pre-school teacher who would come once a week to play with me. She observed what I did and told my mum, 'Don't worry, he's not autistic.' It was the first time the word had ever been mentioned. Diane was my next lifeline and she was my helper in playschool. As I was out of nappies I was allowed to go to playschool twice each week. It meant that if I chose to join in with the other children, or in my case play alongside them, there was a voice to explain why I was doing whatever I did. Diane was a lovely lady. She didn't understand me at all but she was very kind and very patient.

My next step on the road to improvement was at Highfield School in Ely which is a wonderful learning establishment for children with special needs. The headmistress greeted us with open arms at our interview and seemed really keen to have me attend. There seemed to be no question that I might be a problem. She was very kind and understanding and said I would be welcome to go to the school for a few hours initially and then, if I settled in okay, it could be extended. Mum was delighted and relieved and so at the age of three and a half I attended big school. It was nice to feel wanted and only much later were we to discover that the school was in danger of being closed down so the headmistress was on a crusade to boost numbers. We are so glad she was because if the school hadn't been saved I don't know where I would have ended up. More importantly, I don't know where my mother would have ended up!

The school thrived, which is sad in a way because it means there are lots of special needs children around but it has also meant that we recently moved to bigger and better premises. The headmistress is retiring this year but in recognition of her efforts the main hall in the school has been named after her, which is really nice.

Anyway I went and I am still there so I guess I was in the right place at the right time. It was decided that I should have a Statement. This means that all provisions deemed to be necessary for me such as speech therapy, physiotherapy and music therapy written into that Statement have to be provided. It gets reviewed annually but so far I've had no complaints.

I had still not been properly diagnosed which was a bit of a problem when we were out. If I was noisy or acted a bit unusual for a child of my size and age, my mother would find herself explaining my entire life history at great length to complete strangers. It was easier when we thought I was deaf because she would pretend to sign to me. I never did understand what she was attempting to say when she waved her hands around and I'm not wholly convinced that she did either. It looked effective though and saved the lengthy explanations. My problem was that I looked so normal. I was quite cute actually and if you look sweet you can get away with a lot it seems, although I was never deliberately naughty. I was just frustrated and confused – but more about that later.

Okay, at four and a half it was wake-up time. I finally got a label and I guess I drew the short straw because I got autism. That word again. As soon as it was mentioned my mum's shoulders slumped. It's not life threatening but for my parents it was like a death sentence. It was the end of all their hopes and dreams for me. No good job, no family, no future. No one knows what causes autism but it's like a virus in a computer. It screws up the system and takes hours/weeks/years – a lifetime to sort out. The worst thing about that day was the fact that once they were told I had autism they were just given a few A4 sheets of paper which basically said that if I didn't speak by the age of five I probably never would. It was likely that I would become violent and aggressive and eventually have to go into a home because they wouldn't be able to cope with me. They were told to read as much as they could on autism and to go home and get on with it. Good luck and goodbye. Imagine how they felt. I was no different. I was still Jodi but now I was Jodi the autist.

Life went on and Mum read the recommended books on autism. She wished she hadn't as they made very depressing reading. There was nothing positive in any of them unless you count living a normal lifespan positive. At that time autism in the UK was relatively undocumented so the reading material was limited to what had been written by so-called 'specialists' and 'experts' – all heavy going. Now, in 2002, it is much better and you can get information from parents and even autists themselves. It's a much less depressing picture. The National Autistic Society is also very supportive.

One aspect of autism is interesting but whether it falls into the positive or negative category is debatable. We don't lie, which makes us very honest and trustworthy. That's got to be positive. Now couple that with the fact that we supposedly have no understanding of feelings and emotions, especially other people's, and imagine my mum asking me, 'Does my bum look big in this?' That's a negative – big time. I don't appear to know if I upset my mum. If she cries all I do is possibly say 'wet' and get her a handkerchief to wipe the tears. There are no cuddles or words of reassurance and concern.

I haven't mentioned my dad much. That's because he works abroad most of the time and is rarely around. He went away just after I had my grommets and has come and gone ever since. People wonder if I miss him. Well, now I know who he is but for years I didn't acknowledge him any more than I would a complete stranger. He was just like anyone else but he seemed to want to spend time with me even though I ignored him until I wanted or needed something. Now we do more together and are beginning this bonding thing that's supposed to go on between parents and offspring. He loves me apparently, whatever that means.

OK – we can do this bonding thing if you like but you're not driving

When I got my diagnosis in 1993, the statistics said that the chances of getting autism were four or five in every ten thousand and it was more prevalent in boys than girls. In 2000 there was an article in our local paper which said that the rate of children with some form of autism in this county (Cambridgeshire) was four or five in every thousand. Why?

In 1993 my mum didn't know anyone with autism and the only people who had ever heard of it had watched the film *Rain Man* starring Tom Cruise and Dustin Hoffman. They all thought I would be able to memorize the numbers in our local telephone directory. It's something I've never attempted, but ask me anything about videos and that's a different matter entirely. I have almost two hundred and know every word, every movement and every sound effect on all of them. Anyway, Mum managed to find a local couple who had a son about eight years older than me and they kindly agreed to meet us and have a chat. It was encouraging in as much as my parents were given hope that some of the problems which were proving so difficult at the time might fizzle out as I got older. Some did. Incidentally, the boy whose parents we met is now an extremely tall adult and has this amazing ability with dates. If you tell him your date of birth he can tell you immediately what day you were born on and what star sign you are.

There is a local autistic support group called EAST to which my parents were invited just after I was awarded my label. Parents get together and discuss their autistic and Asperger's syndrome offspring and it provides details of where you can get the help to which you are entitled. On their first visit my parents were obviously feeling pretty apprehensive and very vulnerable. The speaker at the meeting had two autistic children himself and was religious. He told the parents that they were special and had been specifically chosen by God to have children with problems. He said God had looked down at all the people in the world and decided which couples would be able to cope. He'd selected them because He knew that they would love their children and look after them. Mum cried.

Being one of the chosen didn't make life any easier. Poor Mum bore the brunt of my frustration and anguish. They say you always hurt the one you love and I must have really loved my mum because I used to beat her up. I'd really hit her and kick her and she never once hit me back. She'd hold my wrists and bend her body back from me in such a way that I couldn't reach her. She'd try to look into my eyes and say, 'No smacking'. To this day, if ever I don't want to do something or go somewhere, I will say, 'No smacking'. I suppose it's my way of saying 'no' but my mum hates it because when we are out she is frightened other people will think she does smack me and she never has. How could she? Autists learn by example so how could she justify telling me not to smack and then turn round and hit me herself? I used to come home from school and hit her or run in from the garden and give her a whack. She never knew why and I could never explain. I never hit anyone else. Mum was my punchbag and it must have been awful. Once I nearly broke her leg. She had taken me for a weekend break to Butlin's in Skegness along with my brother and my grandparents. Something upset me and I kicked her shin as hard as I could. I had roller skates on at the time.

Autism comes in many forms, none of which are pleasant. The range spans from severely autistic through to Asperger's down to the 'anorak'. They make the bearer 'different' and we all know the reaction of the majority of society to that special feature. I've been called all sorts of things and had terribly rude comments made about me when I've been communicating in the only way I knew how. Okay, it wasn't necessarily traditional to throw yourself on the floor and roll around screaming or to kick glass doors, but what else could I do? I couldn't speak, couldn't point, couldn't write, didn't look at people or even at the things I wanted except peripherally. How else could I let it be known that I wanted something? Naturally I got a response and people would make all sorts of rude comments within earshot. One old woman once offered my mum her walking stick because she thought I was being a naughty boy and should be beaten. Poor Mum. She went through so much with me.

I can see and I can hear but the words don't affect me the way they obviously do my family. Just ask my brother Daryl. He's only fourteen, a sensitive child, kind and considerate, but he's had to put up with my strange and unusual behaviour most of his life. He's suffered. He even got into a fight about me at school and if you knew my brother you'd realize how out of character that is. Daryl was defending me from name callers who made a derogatory remark and they didn't even know me. That's the thing about autism. It doesn't just affect the person who has it.

Brotherly love

Once when I was about eight we were on the beach and I was playing in some pools of water left by the tide breaks after the sea had gone out. There were some children with nets and buckets looking for crabs in the same pool. I had been splashing and sitting in the water and got sand in my trunks. It was uncomfortable so I took off my trunks, sat in the water and washed the sand from between my legs. It seemed a sensible thing to do. I didn't bother to put my sandy trunks back on. The children were horrified and kept saying things like 'Yuk', 'That's disgusting'. They went and told their parents and when we walked by the adults made some very rude comments. I guess they probably thought I'd been to the toilet in my trunks and was cleaning off in the water. I couldn't explain otherwise. Mum is not a confrontational person and just gets upset so, although she did offer an explanation, it was not very convincing. She left with 'Ought to be kept locked up' ringing in her ears.

Not that wretched sand again

I'm autistic because apparently I satisfied the Triad of Impairments. My trips to the psychologists were obviously to see which of the criteria on their checklist I fulfilled to get a specific diagnosis. It's a sort of test I suppose and took me almost two years to complete. In July 1993 they decided I had social and communication difficulties and lacked imagination. I was autistic and on a scale of one to ten, with one being the most severe, I rated about a four.

Imagination, now that is a wonderful asset. It isn't just the ability to tell stories. I am thirteen years old and since 1990 I have never played with a toy. I don't know how. If you gave me a farmyard complete with tractors and animals or a garage with lots of cars, all I would do is line up the cows or the cars in very straight lines. They would most likely be grouped according to their colour, size or shape. I know they are smaller versions of the real thing but so what? A car is a car, a toy is a toy. Things are what they are. There is black and there is white. There is no grey, or is there?

Now one thing which is pretty common in autists is heightened sensitivity. It varies from person to person but in extreme cases can mean that a drop of rain falling on your skin feels as though you have been struck by a stone, or the water running gently through pipes can sound like a roaring waterfall. Some autists see, hear and feel everything and it can make the world a very frightening place.

Imagine taking a trip to your local supermarket and visualize yourself walking along the aisle with your trolley. What do you see? What do you hear? What do you smell? You are probably so wrapped up in looking at the prices and the different things on offer that it won't be much. You will concentrate on one thing at a time. The autist, on the other hand, might see, hear and smell everything and all the information will be processed with equal intensity.

There is an autistic lady, Ros Blackburn, who travels around the country giving talks and she has the most articulate and funny stage presence. She recounts her experiences and can hold an audience enthralled for hours. When she talks, people listen. She never actually looks at anyone in the audience but she will come out with comments like 'Will the gentleman sitting on the right-hand side, third row from the back, please stop playing with the tissue in his pocket'.

Once my mum rang her up at home and asked her what she was doing. She said she was sitting in her room looking out of the window and all she wanted to see was the name on the side of the removal van across the road. However, because of her hypersensitivity Ros could see everything with equal intensity.

She saw reflections in the windows, people walking, leaves blowing across the street, trees swaying, animals reflected in car bumpers and traffic moving. She could hear people talking, the noise of traffic, her computer humming, my mum moving paper round at the other end of the phone line and my *Fantasia* video playing on the television in a different room. So much information, it's no wonder she found it hard to concentrate.

Somehow, the autist has to find a way to eliminate some of the distractions. When I watch television sometimes I will get up really close and put my ear against the set. It allows me to hear only what I want to hear. I also tend to frame things up. I will hold up my thumb and my index finger in the shape of an 'L' and look at whatever I want to within that framework, or I'll make a circle and look through it with the other eye closed as if using a telescope. It shuts out what I don't want to see.

I used to hold my hands over my ears as if things were too loud. My parents decided I could be sound sensitive. They heard about the Light and Sound Therapy Centre in London which offered a combined two-week sensory integration programme for people with auditory processing difficulties. Auditory Integration Training (AIT) was common in the USA but relatively new in the UK and there was a long waiting list. It was designed to help individuals overcome sound sensitivities which often result in behavioural and learning disabilities. Combined with light therapy, it was supposed to be quite a therapeutic tool for children with autism. My parents decided to give it a go and set about raising the £1250 required for the two daily half-hour sessions required on the ten-day course. They mentioned it to my grandparents who mentioned it to other family members and pretty soon a fund-raising effort began. Two of my great aunts have a shop in the village where I live and they put up a poster of a train as I have always been a fan of *Thomas the Tank Engine* and steam trains in general. From the funnel there were five clouds of smoke and the idea was that each one would be filled in upon the receipt of £250 until the final target was reached. My mum wrote the following poem to go with it:

Hello, my name is Jodi
I'm the reason for this train
I hope it's going to help me
Get back to your world again.

You see, when I was only small
Doing normal baby stuff
Something happened in my head
My brain said, 'That's enough.'

My world became a scary place
I lived in constant fear
I'd shut out every sight and sound
Allowing no one near.

I saw all kinds of doctors
Psychologists and the rest
I had hearing aids and grommets
All kinds of different tests.

At last I got a label
Not to be wished on anyone
It's nothing to be proud of
AUTISM isn't fun!!!

It means I can't communicate
Don't understand the rules
How to act, what to do
I really get confused.

So if you see me out sometime
Not behaving quite my best
Please don't condemn, but understand
I'm different from the rest.

I have to be taught everything
Unlike other little boys
I have no friends, can't play games
Don't know what to do with toys.

There is no cure they tell us
Which makes Mum very sad
But I'm improving all the time
So things aren't quite so bad.

The therapy in London
Could help me quite a lot
Of course there is no guarantee
But it's the best chance that I've got.

So if you've helped to make the smoke
Rise up from out this train
Be sure that I'll try very hard
To reach your world again.

I cannot speak; I've not the words
To thank you as I should
But maybe soon, who knows?
Now wouldn't that be good!

Cake stalls and whist drives were held. Local charities donated, old people gave their pensions and children handed over their pocket money. The response was incredible and within a month we had the funding. This was just as well because my appointment for December 1995 was brought forward to July due to a cancellation.

We elected to commute to London each day rather than stay, as I was still a difficult child. We had our first half-hour session at 9 o'clock in the morning and then a four-hour break. In the sessions I had to sit in a small cubicle with headphones on and listen to music whilst looking at different coloured lights. It sounds bizarre but when you are sound sensitive certain sound frequencies are heard better than others so you become hypersensitive to them.

A special machine called an audiogram can show these frequencies visually like a range of mountains referred to as 'auditory peaks'. The peaks on each ear are not always the same and as a result the different hypersensitivities in each ear can distort incoming sounds to such an extent that not only is the sound muffled but it can also hurt. The AIT teaches the ears to work in tandem so that the same sounds are heard in each ear – a sort of balancing act. By stimulating the right ear, speech and language are also improved because these are regulated by the right hemisphere of the brain. The light therapy works on the hypersensitivity to bright lights. You look at a coloured disc in a machine for a certain length of time and different colours stimulate different emotions. It is non- invasive and stimulates the brain to improve physical and emotional functions.

Anyway, back to my sessions. In the small cubicle were two chairs and I was supposed to sit on one and the therapist on the other so she could check the audiogram and adjust the sound frequencies and coloured lights accordingly. However, I refused to be prised away from Mum and clung to her in my usual limpet style so it was decided that I should sit on her lap. When the headphones were put on I took them off, so Mum held them on. I struggled and kicked out. I knocked the expensive machine and almost kicked a hole in the wall. Eventually my dad was called in to assist and he held my feet whilst my mum secured me in a vice-like grip with my arms trapped at my side. The half-hour passed but I refused to look at the lights. It was cramped and uncomfortable. Four people squashed in a small space was not very pleasant and I was doing my utmost to make it worse. I am surprised my parents didn't give up there and then.

The afternoon session was much better. We had a different therapist. She was very experienced, super-efficient and stood no nonsense. She actually spoke to me like a grown-up and told me what was going to happen and not what she'd like to happen. I'd never been spoken to like that before. It was a bit like Barbara Woodhouse training dogs. She spoke, I obeyed. My parents couldn't get over it and wanted to bring her home to live with us.

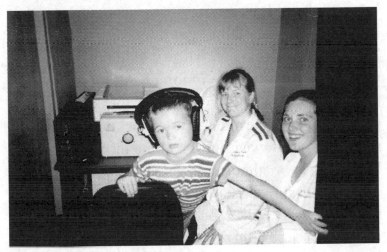

They must be enjoying the music more than I am...

The four-hour break between sessions was very difficult. It was a long time to keep me amused. The weather was good so we were able to go for walks. We would sit in the car outside the centre, eat our picnic lunch and have a drink and then do something else. The first day we managed to find a nice little park within walking distance and I played happily on the slide. It was okay. The next day we went again but we were not alone. A little boy smaller than me came along with his grandfather. Anyway, I was playing on the slide quite happily when this little boy started to climb the steps. He was pretty slow and the first time I gave him space. The next time he was climbing the ladder I'd already had my slide and wanted another go so I got on the steps behind him and gently gave him a push up. It was more of an encouraging nudge really but his grandfather got quite verbal. I suppose he was worried that his charge would fall off and get hurt. Fear makes people ignorant. Although my dad explained I was autistic, couldn't speak and didn't mean any harm, the older gentleman said kids like me shouldn't be allowed out, let alone mix with normal kids. There was almost a bit of slide rage. Adults!

After that we changed locations and would sometimes just walk around. I was okay as long as they kept a close hold on me because I had no sense of danger. Sometimes we would go to McDonald's for some chips. On a good day I wouldn't stand out in there because everyone ate with their fingers. I love the thin fries and will not eat any other kind. My parents have spent many an hour seeking out restaurants which sell thin chips and I have repeatedly embarrassed them by taking other people's off their plates whilst waiting for my order to appear. It's quite extraordinary the reactions you can get.

Shopping was not a good idea with me because I didn't understand that you actually have to pay for things. If I wanted something I just took it and no amount of explaining that it was too expensive would help. One day we were killing time walking along a street when my parents realized I was getting difficult. They frantically searched for an explanation and guessed it might be that we had just passed a toyshop in which there was a steam train. There were big sale notices on the windows so we retraced our steps and went inside. I made a beeline for the train as if drawn by radar because it wasn't visible from the doorway. It wasn't very big actually, but my parents didn't think I needed another train so they put some additional smaller items in the trolley as well with the intention of losing the train before we reached the checkout. I had other ideas. However, when the cashier ran the train through the checkout it came up with a price tag of £119.99. My parents paled visibly. They'd thought it was £19.99 and even that was more than they wanted to spend on what they considered an unnecessary item. Needless to say the train didn't leave the shop – at least not with me. I had to be dragged kicking and screaming from the store and all the way back to the centre. I threw myself on the floor in a tantrum to beat all tantrums. We didn't go shopping again.

By the end of the ten days, my parents were exhausted. Getting up early, all the travelling, the stress of the sessions and additional stress of the breaks in between had taken their toll. Was it worth it? Well, for the first time since becoming autistic I began to say words. I calmed down a bit and began to take notice of things. Small steps but significant. We repeated the process again the following year and this time we found a swimming pool to go to during the breaks which made the whole saga far less stressful.

I used to hate having my nails cut. My mum used to wait until I was in a deep sleep before she did it. Bearing in mind that I didn't sleep much or for long anyway, it meant when she decided to cut my nails she had even less sleep than usual. Apparently, she would wait for hours for the right moment before she dared approach with the scissors. Nine times out of ten I would wake up. Now I am quite happy to have them cut but my mum has to be quick, otherwise I will eat the nail clippings. Waste not, want not. Maybe that is why when I was small I wouldn't have them done – I didn't want to lose part of me. You probably think that is a disgusting habit but how many of you bite your nails?

Another problem I had was with having my hair cut. My mother used to have a mobile hairdresser come round and I'd be sat in front of the video armed with sweets and Hula Hoops. The hairdresser did not dare to use scissors on me because I wouldn't sit still so she used one of those shearing machines similar to the things they use on sheep. It was fast and as long as she didn't drop too much hair on my snacks or block the television I got a decent cut. Sometimes I didn't.

Eventually the hairdresser changed professions so my mum bought a home barber kit and took over. She noticed that when she ran the shearer over certain parts of my head I would try to take the machine off. It seemed to her that it was painful for me. She'd read about another treatment called cranial osteopathy which relieves tension. The brain and the spinal cord are bathed and cushioned by cerebrospinal fluid which should flow freely. Sometimes it gets restricted and can cause physical and emotional problems. Very gentle manipulation by the laying on of hands by a trained therapist can free up those restrictions and allow the body to function better. My parents were willing to give it a try, so in February 1997 I began my treatment.

At the initial consultation my mum told Alex, the therapist, all about me. She warned him that I was autistic, didn't sit still for long, didn't speak much, had little understanding of what was expected of me and hated people touching me. It didn't sound too hopeful. In the room there was a desk, a few chairs and a combi video. That's all I needed to see. Armed with my *Thomas the Tank Engine* video I was happy to take my shoes off and make myself comfortable on the bed. I was not happy to have my head felt though. As soon as Alex put his hands on my head I would remove them.

Practically our entire first session was spent in this pursuit and it was a waste of time and money. As I got used to the system though, I relaxed a bit and allowed him to work on my spine and skull. I had trouble with the two areas either side of my head which had first alerted my mum and wouldn't let him work on them directly so he eased the tension by working via my spine. It just took longer. Eventually after a year it was decided there was little more that could be done to help me so I stopped going. After each session I had seemed much calmer and more alert so it was generally felt to have been useful and I'm okay having my hair cut now.

Guilt and blame are two words that often crop up amongst the parents of autistic children. They wonder if something they did caused the autism. My mum has tortured herself incessantly over my situation, which is silly because it's very negative. You can't turn back the clock. Just before we left Brunei, another couple we knew really well were also leaving and they were having a garage sale. Mum bought this unusual puppet from Bali off them. It was quite large and had a masked face. Four years later she met up with the woman who'd originally owned it. Delia mentioned that she'd never felt comfortable about the puppet and had seemed to have nothing but bad luck after they'd bought it. Since it had gone from their house, their lives had improved. Now my mum says she isn't superstitious but the puppet disappeared immediately. She didn't dare to burn it in case it was an evil spirit so she put it out in the rubbish instead. She hopes no one ever retrieved it from the dump.

Another of her guilt trips concerned *Snow White and the Seven Dwarfs*. When my brother was small and I was still a 'normal' baby we loved that film and indeed still do. My parents used to study us and decide which dwarf we resembled. Daryl became known as Grumpy because he was at the 'terrible two' stage. I became Dopey. He had a cute face and didn't speak. What's new?

Some autists speak, some use the odd word and others don't speak at all. When an autist doesn't speak, other people tend to give them a voice. In doing so, they make decisions for them. They presume to know what the autist wants, why they are doing what they are doing, where they want to go, etc., etc. How often people get it wrong. It's not intentional, of course, but how frustrating it must be for the autists who personally know what they want or need but have no way of communicating it. Imagine if you had suffered a stroke or been in an accident so that you were left with your brain functioning normally but no longer had speech and couldn't write. Oh, and you didn't know the difference between yes and no so you wouldn't be able to nod your head to give a specific answer to an appropriately worded question. How do you think you would let others know what you wanted? It's not easy.

I expect those of you who have very little knowledge of autism may have heard that we all have strange little rituals and obsessive behaviours. This can be the case. I know of children who have to switch every lightswitch on in the house every time they go somewhere and others who lick the windows. There is a girl who would not go on a beach and another who confounded her parents by only going on certain buses. Why? If you were confronted with those situations and the child was unable to offer an explanation, what would you assume?

As it happens, each of these autists was able to reveal the reasons when they got older. The little boy with the lightswitches noted the amount of time it took for the light to come on in each room after he'd pressed the switch. The girl who licked the windows was checking to see what the temperature was outside. The one whose parents thought she must not like the feel of the sand under her feet discovered that she was terrified by the noise of the ocean. The bus problem turned out to be that the girl could not cope with too much of the colour red. She could handle green, blue or yellow buses but not red. By gradually introducing her to the colour in increasingly larger amounts – a handkerchief, a flag, a blanket, a carpet – the problem was eventually overcome and she can now travel on any colour bus.

Patience and persistence. These two words are used a lot in our house. They were introduced to us when my parents discovered the Son-Rise Programme run by the Option Institute in America. It is a two-week programme aimed at encouraging parents to look upon autism as a gift. My mum is still working that one out.

Son-Rise was devised by Barry and Samahria Kaufman, the parents of Raun, who was diagnosed severely and incurably autistic when he was very young. His parents refused to acknowledge what the 'specialists' predicted as Raun's future bleak prospects. They saw through the shield he presented to the world and decided to work with him to help him be the best he could. They had no idea what they would do, how they would do it or how far it would take them. All they knew for certain was that they would not give up on their son. Their ground-breaking programme which is based on love and acceptance is documented in their book *Son-Rise: The*

Miracle Continues and in a movie called *A Miracle of Love*. As a result of their efforts and dedication, Raun is now an articulate, socially interactive young man with a near genius IQ who now teaches the programme to others – not bad for someone who was once a mute, withdrawn child with an IQ of less than 30. He is a real success story and an inspiration. My mother read the book and decided this was to be her next attempt to help me.

A course was to be held in London in July 1998 and my mother attended it. She travelled with another couple who live in a village close by and also have an autistic son. Our families have since become very good friends. The programme was different from any other method of teaching she had ever heard of. Although there was no guarantee of success, it had already helped thousands of families. It is an intense, child-led, home-based programme performed on a one-to-one basis.

Yes, you did read that correctly. The programme is child-led despite the fact that often the child can hardly function. Children are not judged, their behaviour is not labelled as good or bad, right or wrong, appropriate or inappropriate. It is accepted that the child is doing the best he or she can. If they could do it better (talk, care for themselves, interact in more meaningful ways), they would. Instead of insisting that the child conform to what society perceives to be acceptable, attempts are made to enter and understand the child's world. It is hoped that this builds up enough trust to encourage the children to cross over from a world where they feel very safe and secure to one which is, at the very least, confusing.

There are no right or wrong ways to run the programme but suggestions were made about those which had been most successful. Each child is an individual and each set of circumstances is different. As the programme is home-based you have to consider the rest of the family too. It was recommended that children participating in this programme should be taken out of school and volunteers recruited to teach the child. The advantage of volunteers is that they are there because they want to be and not because of some financial gain. The programme works best when the child remains in one room where there are very few distractions and is not allowed out of the house That sounds awful since you actually want the child to interact with everyone, but it makes sense if you consider that, far from actually enjoying outings, most autistic children find them too overpowering, confusing and frightening. Not a good start if you want to encourage them to cross that bridge to 'normality' – whatever that is. The transition has to be gentle and encouraged by people who really care.

My mum attended two separate two-week courses in London, which was pretty expensive, but my parents saw it as a possible investment in the future – both theirs and mine. In August 1998, Mum felt ready to begin.

Volunteers for our programme were duly recruited and emphasis was placed on the fact that the programme had to be exciting, creative and motivational. After all, whatever I was being encouraged to enter had to be more appealing than the safe world in which I found sanctuary.

My programme with volunteers only ran at evenings and some weekends because my parents decided to keep me in school. Their thinking behind this decision was that I was already mixing anyway so it seemed silly to take me away from the very people I was aiming to interact with. Initially, I had five wonderful volunteers who each came for one hour a week, with this number reducing to three during the final months.

We had a room which was designated for my sessions and when the volunteers came we would enter it together and then do whatever I decided I wanted us to do. It was vital that I entered the room willingly. Once inside, I could cry, scream, bang, kick or do anything I wanted, but I had to go into the room on my own volition with no physical contact. It was an invitation and I had a choice of whether I wanted to accept or not.

There was a two-way mirror in the wall through which my mother observed the sessions. She would then give the volunteers feedback on what had happened and what she thought could have gone better or how the volunteers could have reacted in various situations to have more impact. Once a month we were supposed to have a meeting where all the volunteers discussed their sessions with each other and decided what route to take next to try and help me. They all needed to do the same thing in their sessions or at least behave in the same manner in specific situations so that I wouldn't be confused.

My mum had rules for anyone working with me which she gave to all my volunteers and stuck this notice up outside the room as a constant reminder:

PLAYROOM

See the room as the best environment for Jodi to learn in. It could be the gateway to his freedom. Be comfortable and enjoy your time in there. We are *inviting* not forcing Jodi to join us so there should be no physical manipulation.

ATTITUDE

It is very important you are with Jodi because you want to be and not because you feel obliged. When you are with him you must be present, which means you must be concentrating 100 per cent on what you are doing together. You must be loving, accepting and non-judgemental. Be happy, because the happier you, are the clearer you are.

EYE CONTACT

This is probably the most important aspect. It is essential that eye contact is made and retained. This will require body positioning and bringing things to eye level. Eye contact increases attention span, encourages language and is a way of connecting and relating. Looking is learning! Point to your eyes, wear glasses, use face paints.

FACIAL EXPRESSION/VOICE TONE/ LANGUAGE/ BODY LANGUAGE

Jodi is a very intuitive child. He will be able to pick up if you are bored or pretending so it is important that you are enthusiastic about anything you do with him and that you *want to* rather than *have to*. Remember the three Es – **E**nergy, **E**xcitement, **E**nthusiasm.

GRATITUDE/EXPECTATIONS

Be free with praise. Thank Jodi for everything, even just looking directly at you or passing something. Everyone likes to be appreciated.

Remember that Jodi is doing the best he can. If he could do it better he would. Thank him for trying. Celebrate his achievement.

BEHAVIOUR

If Jodi does something not desirable/appropriate such as screaming or banging, please *ignore* it. Do not say things like 'Don't do that', 'Naughty boy', 'No'. Most people do things for a reaction. If you react when he does something wrong he might do it again just to get some reaction. Look away, ignore it completely.

Instead, react when he does something appropriate. Turn everything into a positive. If he writes on the walls, don't say 'Don't write on the walls' but rather, 'That's a lovely picture but let's write on the paper next time'. Show him how much pleasure he can give by doing that.

Instead of telling him what not to do show him what you want him to do.

JOINING/GUIDING

Let Jodi lead in the choice of activities. A happy child will learn more if he is doing something he wants to do rather than something someone else wants him to do. Build on whatever he does. If he lines up trains, add another one. If he names colours, look for things of that colour and then add another one. If he says letters of the alphabet, look for things starting with that letter.

His concentration is very limited so he won't stay at any task for very long. Be flexible and prepared to flit from one thing to another but try to expand the time spent on each individual activity. If Jodi wants to stop doing a jigsaw after three pieces ask him please to put just one more piece in and then say 'Well done' and 'Thank you'.

EXPLAIN

Tell Jodi everything you are doing and why. Talk clearly. Remember that although he doesn't say very much he is nine years old and understands much more than we think. Don't treat him like a baby.

COMMUNICATION

This is a two-way process and the behaviour of one person affects the way the other person reacts. Whatever Jodi does, look at it as though he is trying to tell you something. Even if he is angry and throws a tantrum you should assume he is trying to communicate. He may be bored, angry or even frightened. Be a happy detective. He does everything for a reason. Acknowledge him. Tell him you don't understand what is wrong, what he is trying to tell you, and that maybe if he showed you what he wanted, or said a word it would help. Apologise for not understanding. If he does communicate properly respond *quickly*. If he does it inappropriately act dumb or respond very *slowly*. Always respond if he says '*no*'!

SHARING/TURN TAKING

This is an area which Jodi finds very difficult. Try to encourage this as much as possible and show great enthusiasm and appreciation when he achieves it. Be patient and persistent but be prepared to back off if he says no. Be optimistic. You may attempt something ninety nine times and fail but the hundredth time you might succeed. Vary your approach.

LANGUAGE

Try to encourage language at all times. Jodi will use the minimum to get what he wants, so act dumb. Concentrate on introducing language that will be useful such as nouns, verbs, adjectives and concepts. Demonstrate the words.

Avoid using figurative speech. Jodi tends to take things literally. Do not use phrases like 'Let the cat out of the bag', or 'You are driving me up the wall'.

Be aware of giving mixed messages such as asking for something and accepting something else. If you ask for a yellow Duplo® brick and he gives you a red one, thank him for trying but ask him to please get you the yellow one. Use short sentences and give him key words or visual clues to help him understand what you want.

Treat him as an intelligent nine-year-old and give him choices. Allow him time to respond. Sometimes he gets stuck for words and stamps his foot as if trying to make the word come out. Wait. Do not attempt to say the word for him but maintain eye contact. If he gives up before getting the word out, thank him for trying and say the word yourself.

When talking about Jodi, try to include him in the conversation, or at least explain to him why you are talking about him. Nobody likes to be talked about as if they are not there.

TIME

Jodi has very little concept of time. Give him concrete time blocks. Show him the clock and say 'It is six o'clock and I am going to play with you for one hour until seven o'clock', or 'Yes, we can play with Thomas after we have put the jigsaw away'. Keep to the present as much as possible. Avoid talking about the future or the past as this can lead to confusion.

CREATIVITY

Don't make Jodi responsible for your creativity. Be inspirational and motivated. You want to be alluring to him and give him the learning experience that people are fun to be with and that human contact is the best game in town. Let him know he can trust you and that you can be helpful. Be passionate. If you are going to make a fool of yourself do it in a big way.

Her final instruction was that the volunteers should *have fun*. They did. In fact, they said they probably looked forward to my sessions more than I did. They found them therapeutic and most stayed with me until August 2001 when the programme ended. By this stage I was much improved and I have much to thank Fiona, Carl, Steve, Paul and Jacque for. My mum thanked the final three by way of a poem:

> Turn back the clock a few short years
> To the time when we first met.
> How very far I've come since then
> It's easy to forget.

I was scared of almost everything
I'd shut the real world out
And if I needed something
I'd bang, or kick or shout.

But you decided that you could
Show me another way
So selflessly you took me on
Each week you came to play.

At first it wasn't easy
I wouldn't let you near
Ignoring all you said or did
When clearly I could hear.

But patiently and persistently
Each week one by one
You'd come and see me for one hour
And we would have some fun.

I'd have you leaping up and down
Always seeking out my face
You'd talk and play, try everything
To free me from 'my place'.

And slowly I began to look
My attention span increased
I'd concentrate, participate
And even try to speak.

I know I've still a lot to learn
But you've opened up the door
Thanks to your perseverance
I don't 'ism' anymore.

The weeks and months have come and gone
Now our programme has to end
But just like my precious videos
You're special to me my friend.

I can't help but make more progress
You've given me such a start
I won't forget your contribution
So thank you from my heart.

With much love and gratitude
        JODIxxxxxxx

The Son-Rise programme gave my parents hope and
the results have been spectacular. I rarely ever revert to
my autistic state when I seemingly operate in another

Son-Rise volunteers

world and haven't 'ism'd' for months. I never hit my mum. I make good eye contact and have a far better understanding of what is expected. There is still a long way to go but everyone is on a journey of discovery aren't they?

At this point I should probably explain an 'ism'. For the uninitiated, this is basically a self-stimulating behaviour that gives comfort. For the autist it is a coping mechanism. When the world gets too overpowering we just get into our isms and switch off. So-called 'normal' people have them too when they get stressed. Have you ever seen someone suck their thumb, twiddle their hair, rock in a chair, drum their fingers, or do some deep breathing exercises – how about smoking? Now apart from smoking, most of the activities in this list are socially acceptable, but that is not always the case with the autist. Some of their isms can be pretty weird and tend to get them noticed. 'Normal' people usually make the mistake of trying to stop us doing them, which just makes the whole situation more stressful than ever. It's usually better to leave well alone, although I can well understand that if you were to see a child banging his head rhythmically against a brick wall or the floor you might be tempted to step in. The thing is that child will be banging at the toughest part of his skull where he is least likely to cause himself damage. You could always get him a cushion if it made you feel any better – oh, and move him away from glass windows, just in case! No, seriously, autists don't generally do anything to deliberately hurt themselves although you do get the self-injurious type sometimes and they do need watching. Another favourite 'ism' is spinning round in circles. You may find an autist can do this for hours. Don't worry, they won't get dizzy as their equilibrium is different from yours.

There is always a reason for everything autists do. At one lecture my mother attended she heard of a little boy with encephalitis which is inflammation of the brain. This little boy's ism was to stuff a blanket in his mouth and his parents were naturally concerned about the health implications. Not only could the blanket harbour germs, but also he could have choked. It turned out however that this poor child was looking after himself because whenever he stuffed the blanket against the roof of his mouth it relieved the pressure in his head. DIY acupuncture.

Autists need their isms but if they can be adapted to be more socially acceptable and mobile then all the better. One person I know is addicted to paper. She loves everything about it and will always have some with her. Ideally she likes to flick it in front of her eyes. This can be a bit disconcerting in public so she has small 'flappies', as she calls them, concealed in her trousers and just sticks her hands in her pockets where she can flick to her heart's content. No one even notices.

I love travelling and am very happy to be a passenger in a car or coach. I am less sure about aeroplanes and boats but that may be due to the noise of the engines. When we travel now I look out of the window and recite parts of videos. I particularly like listening to the Disney songs and if ever I get stressed a bit of music seems to work wonders.

When I was small and very autistic my mum worked as a courier delivering parcels for a mail order company. She liked it because she could fit the job around Daryl's schooling. It allowed her to get out of the house, meet other people and basically keep her sanity. Having an autistic child meant my mother felt unable to visit anyone for fear of what I might do and no one came to see us for the same reason. We felt a bit like social outcasts really and my brother missed out on lots of the opportunities most young kids enjoy. My grandparents were great though.

Anyway, back to this courier thing. The parcels used to be delivered to our house and would have to be sorted out into the most economical routes for delivery purposes. They would be loaded into the car in the most convenient position depending upon their size and shape, so the first ones to be delivered tended to get put on the front seat. I always went with Mum on her excursions and sat strapped into my car seat which was in the back on the left-hand side. It meant Mum could keep an eye on me – not that it was really necessary as I never did anything. I just sat mute and still, looking directly in front of me like a stuffed zombie. To try to get me out of this trance-like state my mum would play children's music and audio tapes. I never moved.

One day, however, she was delivering parcels to a house on the main road. It was an awkward place to stop as it was just past a bend and quite busy. She quickly jumped out of the car, ran to the door and was just getting a signature for her delivery when she heard a squeal of brakes. She turned in horror to find me standing next to her, the driver's side door wide open and a car pulling slowly round it with a very concerned and obviously thankful driver at the wheel. For whatever reason, I had decided I no longer wanted to sit still in the car. As the child locks were on the back doors and the front passenger seat was cluttered with parcels I escaped from the only door available to me – the driver's. I obviously had no idea of the danger to either myself, the car or the other road users. My mum handed in her notice immediately and went back to feeling like a social outcast.

Round about that time my dad was offered a married accompanied position in Oman. My parents wanted to be a proper family again but were concerned as to whether they would be able to cope. Oman is not renowned for its special needs facilities although the country is very child orientated. As in most Middle Eastern countries, anyone with a disability remains hidden. Families deal with the problem within their houses. You never see a disabled person outside. It may have changed now. I don't know.

We decided to risk it and made arrangements with the UK schools that we would go on a three-month trial and see if we liked it. By this time the demand for Highfield School exceeded the amount of places, so my parents were concerned that if things didn't work out I would lose mine. We tentatively put up our house for sale. There was a slump in the market at the time and property wasn't moving so we didn't expect anything to happen. One week after we'd left we had a cash offer for the price we'd requested but the buyers wanted to move in long before we intended to return to the UK. At this stage things were going well in Oman and we thought it would be the start of a new family life together so we decided to sell. My grandparents came to the rescue and packed up the entire house and moved us into rented accommodation. It was no easy feat as the only items that had been removed from the house when we left on our three-month holiday were a few clothes.

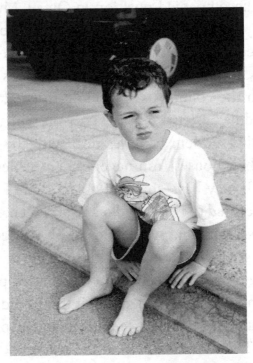

That's enough sitting still – what can I do now?

As it happened things did not work out. I made life impossible for everyone and it was felt the best thing to do would be for Mum to bring Daryl and me back to the UK and Dad would look for another job. If he stayed with his current one it meant that he had a nice house to live in but never got back to England as we were supposed to be out there with him. It was bad enough for my mum and brother not to see him very often, but not to see him at all was just too much. We could, of course, have gone to visit him but it was expensive for three of us to fly. My brother was still young and I was not the best of companions on a four thousand mile journey. Airport departure lounges were hell.

We arrived back in the UK to a new address. The house my grandparents had managed to get for us was in the village where they lived and where my mum had grown up so that was fine. It was on three levels with a lovely cellar which held the items we didn't need and all our toys. On the ground floor were the kitchen, hall and lounge/diner and upstairs were three bedrooms and a bathroom/toilet. It was nice but completely unsuitable for me because I used to climb on anything and everything. My sense of balance was incredible which is probably why I was able just to get on a bike and ride it. My parents always said they thought I could walk on a washing line. Fear was something which I apparently lacked and, coupled with no sense of danger, for me the steep stair banisters held great appeal. One slight slip from the glossy two-inch handrail and this story would never have been written.

Another area of concern was the beautiful old stained glass window at the top of the stairs. This was great to hit so Grandad covered it with a thick sheet of perspex which reduced its visual impact considerably. We had arrived back in the UK on the Wednesday and by Saturday we were in the process of buying a new property. My mum went straight to the estate agents and bought the first house she looked at. Six weeks later we moved in and her first job was to have toughened glass put in every window.

I have mentioned my apparent lack of fear. This also applies to water so I never had to be taught to swim. I could do it. I suppose it never occurred to me that I might drown. That's all very well except that I was a nightmare to take anywhere near water because I loved it so much. I didn't care if it was a small puddle or a deep river. I loved the sea too and would always want to go in for a paddle, irrespective of the weather.

One cold, windy day in April my parents took my brother and me for a refreshing stroll along Hunstanton seafront. It was bracing to say the least. Now Hunstanton has an amazing beach. It is very flat and you can go out for miles sometimes and the water never gets beyond your knees (if you are an adult).

Having a splashing time – glad you're not here

Somewhere in the distance I spotted an orange buoy in the sea and I ran for it. I was and still am fast. Although my mother had her trusty trainers on, it was decided that my dad should chase after me as he is much fitter. I ran and he followed thinking I would stop when I reached the water's edge. I didn't. I just waded in and made a beeline for the orange buoy which was bobbing around like a ball, inviting me to come and throw it. My dad stopped on the shoreline and took off his socks and shoes, quickly rolled up his trousers and headed into the cold spring sea. By the time he caught up with me the water was as high as my chest and above his knees. He was frozen. I wasn't. (That's another thing I never used to feel – the cold. I have been known to walk around in the snow with no socks or shoes and not be in the slightest bit fazed. Now I want them all – socks, boots, hat, gloves, the lot.) Fortunately, my parents had the foresight to take a change of clothing for me as they had learned from previous excursions that if I got my clothes even the slightest bit wet I would take them off. (When we were in Oman we once went to a restaurant and I spilled my drink down me so I stripped off. In a Muslim country this was not such a good idea.) When we left the beach I was clean and dry and my dad was cold and wet. He got some really strange looks from people who must have thought 'What an idiot going into the sea this weather'. If only they knew.

I was assigned a lovely social worker in the days when their workload wasn't so great and funds not so stretched. Suzie was very interested in me as I was a bit of a novelty. She was extremely astute and worked out long before my mother that respite care would be extremely beneficial for us. My mum was utterly opposed to the suggestion because she felt it was a reflection on her ability to cope. However, Suzie pointed out that for the most part we were a one-parent family and my brother Daryl needed quality time as well. He had to be able to do the things 'normal' people do like go for walks, shopping trips or visits to the cinema. Suzie retired as a social worker a couple of years ago but if you ever see her walking around you will recognize her from the halo glowing above her head.

Respite care came in the form of 204 Norwich Road which is a fabulous house for children with special needs. It is just like a home from home and exactly twenty miles from our house. When Suzie took my mum to visit it for the first time and talk to the staff she was very impressed. It was clean and comfortable and the staff were very welcoming and friendly. She had reservations though. I couldn't communicate in any recognizable form at that stage so if I was abused how would she know? Also, she'd never left me with anyone other than my grandparents since I'd become autistic and only then for a few hours at the most. How would I cope, and more importantly, how would she?

Suzie worked on her and initially I went for a few hours and this gradually built up to overnight stays twice each month. In the school holidays I stay for longer. At first I climbed on everything and distanced myself from everyone. No one could tell how I felt about going but they assumed I didn't mind because over a period of time I changed from having to be prised away from my parents to actually saying 'Bye' and pushing them out of the door. Until very recently I took a selection of videos with me every time I went

– about thirty – and I also used to sleep with one in my bed. I suppose it was my version of a cuddly toy.

There was one period when I didn't appear to want to go to respite care. It only lasted for two sessions but on the Saturday mornings when my parents were due to take me I ran away. We have big wrought iron gates which are secured with a dog chain. The idea is to keep me in. They don't work.

On the first Saturday morning when I escaped my parents had been busy packing up the car and left me happily (or so they thought) watching a video in my bedroom. When they had completed their task they came to get me and I was nowhere to be seen. Searches of the bedrooms, downstairs rooms and garden proved fruitless. Mum went upstairs to have a double check in case I had hidden under the bed or in the wardrobe. Through the landing window she happened to spot a little figure running along the river bank. She felt sick. The figure was obviously me and in order for me to be where I was I would have had to get out of the locked gates, make my way along a busy road, cross a railway line, climb over a stile and run beside a very deep river.

If I carried on in the direction I was going I would come to another stile which led into someone's garden where there were some dogs. I was terrified of dogs and have been known to leap into the arms of complete strangers when I've seen one. She was frightened that if I encountered one I would leap straight into the river and the next time she saw me I'd be dead.

If I managed to get through the garden unscathed I would come to another branch of the same river and then onto a very busy road. At this point, if I turned right I would head towards the bypass and if I turned left I would cross the main railway line to London. They were all known dangers, but what if someone grabbed me? It didn't bear thinking about.

She leapt down the stairs as fast as she could, shouted a garbled message to my dad that he had to take the car to the station and head me off so I couldn't get onto the main road and then set off after me in hot pursuit. It would probably have been wiser to send my dad on foot as he is much fitter but there was no time to think. She ran but I ran faster and I had a good headstart so she was never going to catch me. The most she could hope for was to block me off if I decided to retrace my steps.

As it happened, I didn't get the chance because when I made my way through the garden and past the boats moored on the river there stood my dad. Apparently my face was a picture. Mum's was too – red, hot and sweaty! The next time I tried it my parents were more prepared and Dad caught me almost as soon as I'd scaled the front gates. For months afterwards I was not allowed outside on my own and

kept continually in sight. The neighbours were also
primed that if they saw me outside the gates they
should do something about it – fast.

After that I seemed to accept the situation and now
I even pack my own bag. It no longer contains videos.
I was made very welcome at 204 Norwich Road. My
family enjoy the break and everyone is happy. At
Christmas Mum wrote them a poem. They were
touched to read these words:

> As we all pass through our lives
> Many people we will meet
> Some we'll get to know quite well
> Others just to greet.
>
> Sometimes these acquaintances
> Turn into special friends
> People you can really trust
> On whom you can depend.
>
> I've found such friends at 204
> You're exceptional I find
> All generous and helpful
> Considerate and kind.

I've had respite now for quite some time
And when I reach the door
You welcome me with open arms
Of that I can be sure.

So many different children
But it's like a home from home
Each child gets attention
And no one feels alone.

There's never any pressure
I'm allowed to do my thing
You invite me to participate
And sometimes I join in.

Although I don't say many words
I am happy and have fun
You give me all I want and need
So 'thank you' everyone.

Now in this season of goodwill
Christmas greetings I will send
To all of you at 204
Each one a 'special' friend.

MERRY CHRISTMAS
AND HAPPY NEW YEAR

Videos have always played a big part in my life. I suppose I like them because I can rely on them always to be the same. No matter how often I watch them, the story, the language, the actions, the expressions never change. There are no surprises. In a world where everything is changing and confusing that can be a comfort and it is not unusual for autists to really like videos. However, there are two trains of thought about videos in the autistic camp. The experts and specialists say they should be banned completely but the parents usually think otherwise. The argument from the anti-video camp is that they encourage repetitive behaviours. The reply from the parents is usually that they give them a much needed break and since autists have so little by way of enjoyment it seems unfair to deprive them of what small pleasure they do have.

Who needs toys when there are videos?

As mentioned earlier I have quite a collection. Over the years they have cost my parents a small fortune and caused a lot of anxiety but I love them. TV just doesn't do anything for me and although I am encouraged to watch it with 'the rest of the family' I can't wait to get away. If I am encouraged to share TV viewing time I tend to be a bit of a nuisance because I chatter the whole time. As I don't speak very clearly, no one really knows what I'm on about. My brother tells me to 'shut up' but my mum tries to distract me by talking about what's happening. This makes things a whole lot worse for anyone else in the room as they then have two people chattering. My mum knows that I need my video 'fix' every day but she is sensible enough to limit my viewing times. She allows me the same time with the videos as she allows my brother with the TV. That's only fair isn't it?

I love Disney films and have most of them in my collection but when I was small I also liked *Spot*, *Fireman Sam*, *Postman Pat*, *Pingu*, and my beloved *Thomas the Tank Engine*. Later I progressed to *Sooty*, *Rosie and Jim*, *Tots TV*, and *Brum* to name a few. My mum approves of these because although they are for small children and have puppets in them, they cover real life situations so are actually very educational. I often take phrases from the videos and use them in the right context. We have a caravan and last year we stayed on a lovely site in Derby close to Alton Towers.

The site was next to a reservoir and set amongst trees. On the first day of our holiday I sat looking out of the window and uttered, 'So this is Sherwood Forest?' The reply in *Robin Hood* is, 'Yeah, I guess so', but all I got from my parents was an amazed laugh. I've also learned how to kiss by watching videos. If I am told to give someone a kiss I put my head down and thrust it under the person's nose. I've seen Snow White kiss the top of all the dwarfs' heads like that so it must be right.

So this is Sherwood Forest?

Videos – yes I love them. If ever we go shopping I seem able to smell them and even in strange cities you can guarantee I will drag my parents into a shop which sells them although they are not visible from the road. In the past this was a major problem because if I saw a video I wanted I had to have it. I had no understanding of money or paying for things so if I didn't get it there would be a tantrum. If there was more than one I wanted then I had to have them all which played havoc with the credit cards. The worst thing was that if I got the video and then saw it in a shop the next week I would want it again and then again and again. I always wanted to buy the ones I already had in my collection and did not take kindly to being refused. It took years before I understood that the ones in the shop weren't mine and that when I got back home my versions would still be where I'd left them.

Just after Christmas in 1998 before I reached this level of understanding, my mum did some very clever detective work and realized I wanted a new *Thomas the Tank Engine* video which had just been advertised on television. My dad was away and not due home until a few days after Christmas so all his presents had been left under the tree. My mum noticed that I had opened all those resembling the shape of a video and had said 'Thomas chases'. The advertised video was called *Thomas the Tank Engine and Friends, Chases, Races and Runaways*. As I hadn't received it for Christmas she guessed I was trying to tell her I wanted it. On 29 December she rang Woolworths to see if they had it and asked them to save her a copy. She told them she would be down to collect it in half an hour as she knew I still had difficulty queuing and waiting.

When we arrived the shop was extremely busy with people looking for sales bargains and generally walking off the Christmas turkey. My mother, brother and I went straight to the music/video counter and requested the video but by the time the assistant brought it I had wandered off to look at the videos on the rack in the aisle. Daryl came with me. I found two videos I liked and took the boxes to the counter. I already had one of the videos so my mum didn't really want to buy it, but the other was new to me. Although she didn't actually want to buy two videos, she was prepared to let me have them. She explained to the assistant that she would buy the Thomas video we'd ordered and the one I hadn't got, but she didn't want the third as I already had it at home, so could the girl just 'lose it'.

The assistant duly rang up the prices, my mother paid and the requested videos were put in the bag. I realized that there were only two so I waited for the third to be handed over. When it wasn't I leant over the counter to see where it was. I couldn't see it so I climbed up further, almost knocking over a display of CDs in the process. The assistant panicked and my mother tried to get me off the counter by pulling on my coat but this wasn't fastened so it came off in her hands. Meanwhile I was almost over to the sales side so she thrust the videos and coat into my brother's hands and grabbed me.

Now I am strong and was not going to be thwarted so I resisted and knocked her flat on her back in the aisle. By this time a large crowd had gathered to see what all the fuss was about and everyone stared. Everyone, that is, except my brother who had been so embarrassed by my antics that he had left the shop pretending not to know us. My mum picked herself off the floor, came towards me smiling at everyone and told the assistant she would have the other video after all. Much to her credit she kept herself together until she'd retrieved me from the other side of the counter, paid for the video I didn't need and got me safely back to the car. Then she broke down and cried. She also vowed to buy a long blonde wig and never go back to Woolworths again. My brother disowned me.

That Thomas *video must be here somewhere...*

I have mentioned my love of Disney films, particularly the older ones. One school holiday my mother was feeling very brave and decided to take my brother and me to the cinema. *Lady and the Tramp* was showing and as it was one with which I was familiar she thought I might be okay. She wisely chose a mid-week session when she hoped there would not be too many people around. The cinema we go to is very old and has what my mum calls 'character'. We left it until almost the last minute before we bought our tickets because having been told I was going to watch *Lady and the Tramp* I would not have been at all interested in the pre-film trailers. Good move. Consequently, when we went into the actual cinema it was very dark so we sat down as quickly as we could fairly near the front. By the time the film ended we were at the back. I was fine to start with but as the film progressed it became increasingly obvious that as I knew all the words and sound effects I was going to utter them.

'Shush' didn't work because I saw no difference between the cinema and home. I was allowed to do it there, in fact I was positively encouraged to show off my talent, so why not here? Mum tried her best to keep me quiet by plying me with drinks and Polo mints (circles again) but I lined them up on the seat next to me. When it suddenly shot up because I removed my coat to make more space, they all went on the floor. Waste not want not – so I crawled under the seats to get them and whatever else I could find down there. The woman sitting in the seat in front was not amused. The worst part though – at least for my brother – was when I decided to be Tramp and chase a pretend rat down the aisle on all fours, barking. Daryl moved seats and we didn't see him again until the film had finished and the cinema was empty.

I like familiar things and used to be very resistant to change. It is less of a problem now but when I was smaller I would only wear grey jogging bottoms with my jumper tucked inside and my socks pulled up over the elasticated legs. I always looked as though I'd just got off my bicycle. It was really strange and made me stand out even when I was behaving well. An instructor at one of the Son-Rise courses my mother attended suggested it might be because at some stage an ant or something had crawled up my leg or maybe the wind had blown up my trousers and I hadn't liked the sensation. By dressing as I did I was ensuring that nothing could get to me. It's an interesting theory.

When my brother and I were younger my parents dressed us alike and many people mistook us for twins. They still do sometimes (much to Daryl's annoyance) although we no longer wear the same clothing. One advantage of being dressed alike was that I could have Daryl's clothes when he grew out of them. I would wear them quite happily because I was familiar with the style, texture, colour, etc. Now, because we no longer wear the same things, I won't wear Daryl's hand-me-downs as I associate them with him. If they suddenly appear in my wardrobe they quickly find themselves back in his room.

I might wear the gloves but you can forget the rest

There are some clothes that I simply will not wear and this appears to be because of the colour and the texture. Yellow is a definite no. I am getting better with different types of material because over the years we have painstakingly desensitized me by brushing different materials against my skin and encouraged (not forced) me to feel anything and everything. I can even tolerate soap on me, now but for years I couldn't bear it. If I shared a bath or shower with a member of my family I didn't allow them to have it on their skin for long either. My speed with the rinsing water added new meaning to the phrase 'a quick wash down'.

Getting me dressed in the mornings was a major problem because I hate to be rushed and if I decided, for whatever reason, that I was not going to wear the attire that had been chosen for me then I would struggle and protest both physically and verbally. My parents therefore always allowed plenty of time for the dressing ritual and initially made a game of it. If I protested too much they just left me to it and pretended they didn't care if I went around naked. Sometimes this ploy worked and I would attempt to dress myself, but if it didn't and the taxi was about to arrive to take me to school they would allow me to wear my favourite clothes. Although there is a uniform, the variety of the children's disabilities is such that not all can wear it so Highfield School is pretty lenient.

I am past all that now because I will wear my school uniform with no problem and when I am not at school I choose the clothes I want. I will wear a variety of clothes but this took a long time to achieve. If time was tight I was always dressed in my favourite clothes but if we had plenty of time new ones were introduced. Initially all I had to do was put them on, pose for a few minutes, be admired profusely and then take them off again. When we went on holiday or if I went to respite care, different clothes appeared as that way I couldn't dive into my wardrobe and pull out my old favourites. As a precaution, in the early days, old faithfuls were packed in the bottom of the suitcase just in case I decided that if I couldn't wear what I wanted then I'd just go without.

I favour blue and, rather than make a big issue out of clothes, my mum tends to buy items for me in slightly different styles and shades of that colour. This way I'm happy and other people don't think I have only one set of clothes to wear. I change them every day and as I put my dirty pants, socks, trousers, etc. in the linen basket I always make a point of telling my mum 'washing'.

Shoes were also a major problem and my mum dreaded the trips to shoe shops. Apart from the usual wait for the sales assistant, there were the issues of me not wanting to have my feet measured and not letting anyone physically touch me to try on new shoes. If my parents were lucky enough to get past those hurdles, there was then the problem of knowing which shoes I would wear. When they finally found a pair which I was happy with they were very tempted to get them in every size possible so that as my feet grew they could just introduce a larger pair. They usually went for shoes which had blue in them somewhere as that is my favourite colour.

Other problems arose if I was ill. Fortunately, apart from my autism I have been very healthy, which is just as well because I had no way of telling anyone how I felt or which bit hurt. My parents always knew if there was something wrong with me because I would just lie around and hold my head and say 'Ooh'. That didn't necessarily mean I had a headache but gave an indication that something was wrong somewhere. Once the doctor sent me to the hospital because of suspected appendicitis and it turned out that I was constipated.

Another time I clearly had an ear infection as there was green liquid running out of my ear so my parents took me to the doctor. I had to wait in a busy, crowded waiting room which I found incredibly difficult. My appointment time came and went and I was climbing on the chairs, banging the toys on the tables and generally charging around with Mum (still wearing her trainers) chasing me like a shadow and casting apologetic looks at all the people in the room. It's a strange place, a doctor's waiting room. I realize that people who go there are supposed to be sick but no one ever looks at anyone else or speaks, do they? It was so quiet but I soon changed that.

Unfortunately my burst of noisy activity meant I tripped and lost my balance. I hit my eye on the corner of the waiting room where two walls met and it poured with blood. Panic ensued of course but the good thing was that I no longer had to wait to see the doctor. It's not a tactic I would recommend if you are fed up with waiting for your appointment though – I had to have my eyelid stitched and you can imagine how I reacted to that. It took three people to hold me down whilst the doctor repaired my eye and I have a lovely scar to prove it. Since getting my label things have improved because now when I need to see the doctor my parents explain that I am autistic and I'm generally seen straight away.

Well – it took my mind off the ear infection!

Over the years we have done some role play concerning trips to the doctor and dentist using toy medical kits. I also have a really good *Topsy and Tim* video which deals with potentially sensitive situations like going to the dentist, doctor and hospital, as well as other things like going to school, moving house, going on holiday, etc. My mum says the experts can keep their opinions on videos. She finds some of them very useful.

Mum always explains what is going to happen when I have to go somewhere and now I don't mind visiting the dentist or the doctor, especially as I don't have to wait long to see them. Sometimes we go there for no other reason than a chat and that is a good way to allay any fears. Once an autist gets the idea that they aren't necessarily going to be manhandled or hurt if they visit these places, then a lot of the stress is relieved. I usually do a self-examination in both places and the dentist and the doctor allow me to use some of their instruments. I am a dab hand at manoeuvring the little round mirror in my mouth and know how to check my ears, chest and blood pressure. I always say 'Thanks dentist' or 'Thanks doctor' when I leave, even if they don't actually do anything. On the two occasions I have had to have teeth removed (because the baby ones refused to drop out despite my second teeth coming through), I went to the hospital. This was a good tactical move because it means I don't associate my normal dentist with anything nasty or frightening. The hospital was brilliant but I had to have gas to put me to sleep and was a bit sick and groggy afterwards.

Actually I rarely appear to be ill. Sometimes I feel sick and I say 'sink', get a sick bowl and a towel and just get on with it. I don't make a fuss and if it wasn't for the fact that I change my clothes sometimes my mum might not even know I was ill. I have been known to be sick in the middle of the night and when my mum came to see why the light was on and I was moving around she found me stripping the bed ready for 'washing'.

Autists appear to have a very high pain threshold and when I was younger I never cried if I hurt myself, even if it was apparent to everyone else that whatever I had done must have been really painful. My mum always said that if I broke my leg and she rubbed it, kissed it and said 'All better' I would be able to walk on it. I'm not sure if that is good or bad. There are reports of autists who have suffered something so incredibly painful (i.e. broken bones or appendicitis) that had they been 'normal', they would most surely have passed out. Instead they have been temporarily cured of their autism. Don't ask how or why but it seems the normality only lasted as long as the intense pain. Fascinating don't you think?

I don't speak much, at least not clearly, but with the very few words I do use I can convey a lot – at least I can if everyone else is playing happy detective. One day my parents took my brother and me for a picnic in the woods. It was very much another of those split family outings where two of us went one way and the other two another. We were rarely ever able to do something as a foursome.

This particular day I wouldn't venture past the river so whilst Daryl and Dad set off to walk through the trees and check out the wild life – deer, squirrels, rabbits – Mum and I sat on the river bank. Well, she did. I was actually in the shallow, fast-flowing river throwing stones and making a splash. It was a nice afternoon and we watched many people cross the bridge to the actual woods. We also saw them come back again because I could never be rushed and would only stop doing something when I was ready.

Surely it's not time to go yet? I've only been in here a couple of hours...

This was a problem because it meant that sometimes we would spend a lot of money on entrance fees to go somewhere and I'd be ready to leave in five minutes or, alternatively, if I was enjoying myself I'd refuse to leave. One summer in Devon we went to a swimming pool. It was a lovely place with several pools, slides and things and I thought it was great. Obviously lots of other people did too because it was very busy and you were given a coloured wristband to wear when you went in which allowed you an hour in the pool. When your colour was called you had to get out. Those were the rules – but they just weren't mine. We only went there once.

Back to the picnic and once I'd finally decided I would go back to the car we all had something to eat and drink. My dad and brother had been for their walk and had been waited around for ages whilst I was paddling so they were ready for refreshments. Afterwards I needed to go to the toilet and conveyed this message by saying 'tortoise'. My parents were aware of the unusual meaning of this word because I had uttered it several times on a long car journey and been ignored. I therefore took matters into my own hands and released myself from my car seat and pulled on the handbrake. It is not a good idea when you are driving along a busy road but they got the message.

I have been lucky I suppose because I managed to get through the toilet training stage with no problems.

Many children take years to master the skill and there are various strategies which can be applied to assist. One is to make a toilet diary where you give your child a certain amount to drink and then note how long it takes before your child has to pass it. You do this for about a week and then, just before you know your child is ready to relieve him or herself, you jump in with the pot or lead them to the toilet. You do this with a big smile on your face and make it seem as though going to the toilet (in the toilet) is a wonderful, exciting, joyous experience.

You see some children might actually be frightened that they will slip into the toilet bowl and be flushed away like the paper, or they might hate the noise of the water flushing or the feel of the toilet seat against their bare bottom. They might feel that if they part with their faeces it would be like giving some of themselves away so they hold on to it as long as possible. There are all sorts of reasons why autistic children find toilet training so difficult so you really have to get to know your child and persevere until you solve the problem.

I tend to go to the toilet about two or three times a week which probably isn't wonderful, but when you consider my diet and the lack of fruit and vegetables it is okay. I do get grumpy when I need to go and my mum is considering giving me liquid paraffin and sodium picosulphate to see if that will help. Some children get food compacted inside and when that happens all sorts of toxins build up so it might be worth a try.

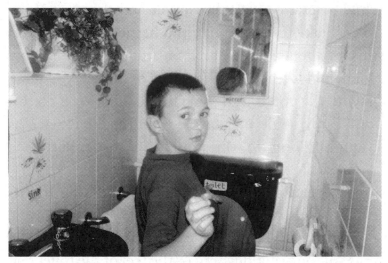

Excuse me – I'm busy

Now going to the toilet when we are out is getting to be a bit of a problem because of my size. Mum used to be able to take me into the ladies' section, but as I get older and bigger it is not really appropriate. I do know I should use the men's section and am perfectly capable of managing on my own, even to wash my hands afterwards, but you just never know who I might meet in there. If my dad or brother are with me it's okay but when I'm on my own with Mum she feels compelled to hover outside the toilet door. She's worried that one day she'll either get propositioned or accused of loitering with intent. Whenever possible I use the disabled toilets.

Anyway, I've digressed yet again, so back to the picnic. After we had emptied our bladders we decided to go home, unpack the car and relax. My parents busied themselves with washing out the flasks and putting things away when they became increasingly aware of me telling them something. I kept looking out of the window and saying 'car'. They replied joyfully that, yes, we had been in the car and had a lovely day at the woods, etc., etc. so once more I said 'car'. I kept repeating the word and then tried 'chicken'. Still no response, at least not the one I wanted so I added 'key' and, just for good measure, 'please'. What more could they possibly need?

Obviously a lot because despite telling them 'car, chicken, key, please' I still had to go outside myself, unlock the car and retrieve my packet of chicken and chip flavoured snacks which had been left in the boot. It's true, if you want something done you just have to do it yourself!

Language is incredibly important for autists and you have to be very specific when you give instructions. I am sure you have heard the stories about *not* saying 'Go and wash your hands in the toilet'. We tend to take things literally and don't always get the implied meanings. Sometimes we are also unable to compensate if things don't exactly go to plan.

There is a story about a young autistic girl who was starting a new school to which she had to travel by bus. She had been on buses before so it was not a new experience. However, her parents were a bit anxious about the first day so her mother told the girl she would follow in the car and that her daughter was to get on the bus, go straight to the back seat and sit down so that she could wave to the girl all the way to school. What the mother didn't tell the girl was what to do if there was someone already sitting there. Whoops!

In her talks on autism, Ros often refers to incidents which illustrate the difficulties of not understanding implied meanings or not being specific. Simple things like directing an autist to sit down can be difficult: 'Take a seat' – where to? 'Sit down' – where? 'Rest your legs' or 'Take the weight off your feet' both suggest sitting down, but most autists need specifics. Ros is mad about trampolining. She goes as often as she can but needs assistance in getting there. Once a woman she barely knew offered to take her so Ros gratefully accepted. She was taken to a class which she attended regularly so knew the set-up and the instructors. This new helper decided that she would also like to have a go at trampolining and asked Ros if she could go and change her clothes. Ros said she could but when the assistant returned to the hall a few minutes later she found Ros in a terrible state. The reason? The woman hadn't told her she was coming back.

Most autists find time-related issues difficult. That is probably why I ran away when I was due to go to 204 Norwich Road on the two occasions previously mentioned. I had no way of knowing if or when my parents would return for me. I am not so bad now because I know the days of the week and can count up to ten so when I go to respite care on Saturday and am told I am going for 'one sleep' and will be collected on 'Sunday' it makes sense.

My mum is always careful to tell me exactly what is going to happen, but not too far in advance so I don't get confused. She speaks in simple sentences, looking directly at me and giving only the relevant information. She always ends her chats with 'Okay?', which I repeat. She's still not sure whether that is just echolalia on my part or whether I am saying 'I understand'.

Mum always makes sure she does what she says she will do. For instance, if she tells me we are going to the shop to buy a newspaper and then going to grandma's house, that's exactly what we will do. If we have to go somewhere else in between or do it in reverse order, she will explain what is happening and why. You know those diversionary tactics some parents employ by using expressions like 'in a minute', 'soon', and, 'after I've done this', to get out of doing whatever it is their offspring want them to do, well, if my mum uses any of those expressions she means them. An autistic child won't wait for long so if they communicate in some meaningful way that they want you to do something you should respond quickly. Hence 'in a minute' should mean exactly that.

It is very important that autists can believe what they are told and trust that when a person says something will happen it does, otherwise it can cause unnecessary distress. The following story serves to illustrate how important clear, precise information is to an autist, irrespective of his or her obvious intelligence and ability.

My mum recently organized a talk to be given by Ros Blackburn on autism at Highfield School. Our friends Rick and Jane volunteered to collect and return Ros safely home, a distance of some seventy miles from us. They have an autistic son and know a lot about autism so they felt comfortable with the situation.

Prior to the journey Rick and Jane spoke to Ros at some length on the telephone so she could get to knew them a bit as spending time with complete strangers in a confined space can be daunting at the best of times and much worse if you happen to be autistic. Ros also wanted to know whether they had a dog and whether one had been in the car as she hated them. She also asked whether they smoked or had smoked in the car. Satisfied that the car would not cause any sensitivities, they arranged a collection point and time, discussed how they would be seated in the car and the route and approximate time it would take to get to Ely where Highfield School is situated.

Rick was not quite sure how to get back onto the motorway from Ros's house so he suggested they follow the Stansted signs, which was fine until he got to the roundabout leading onto the M11 because then he had to follow the signs for Cambridge. He didn't explain to Ros that they weren't actually going to Stansted so she became quite distressed as they appeared to be going in the wrong direction.

I suppose all sorts of things must have crossed her mind including, possibly, kidnap. After all Rick and Jane were complete strangers to her, but whatever they may be (and they are very, very nice) they are definitely not kidnappers. Now Ros is incredibly literate and can communicate very well but at this point she was so distressed that she lost her power of speech and could only point and make strange noises.

Fortunately, Rick and Jane quickly realized there was a problem and were able to reassure her by explaining that they no longer needed to follow the Stansted signs but head for Cambridge instead. They also realized the need to explain when they got closer to their destination that they didn't actually need to go to Cambridge either and would then follow the Ely signs. At that point the cathedral should be visible across the flat fen countryside so they hoped that would provide all the reassurance she needed to confirm they were indeed heading in the right direction for the talk she was due to give.

It did. Ros checked out the cathedral, gave a wonderful talk and was returned safely to her home having first enjoyed a meal at McDonald's. Obviously a woman with great taste!

One form of speech I do indulge in is echolalia. This is the repetition of the last word or phrase spoken so if my mum wants to encourage me to really think about language she will put the word she expects me to say at the beginning of a sentence. For instance, if my mum were to ask me what colour straw I wanted from a choice of 'blue, yellow or red', using echolalia I would say 'red', but if I want my favourite colour blue I have to work a bit harder.

My parents have mixed feelings about me acquiring language. It is no good having lots of words if you don't comprehend what they mean. If you can speak then people generally expect you to be equally proficient in other areas. As you should by now be aware this is not the case with autists. However, this is a verbal society and it is easier to get on if you can communicate in a manner which most people can understand so we will persevere. One autistic girl apparently didn't speak until she was quite mature, when for some reason she suddenly replied to a question asked of her very clearly and precisely. The amazed recipient of her reply asked her why she'd never spoken before and she replied, 'No one ever told me I had to.'

One sunny afternoon my parents took my brother and me for a 'family' walk around the village. Actually it was more of a route march as I am not renowned for going slowly. It's odd because I never appear to be walking quickly so I must take long strides. I am always being instructed to 'slow down'. We ended up in sets of twos with Mum as my chaperone. Dad and Daryl were most likely discussing football and had lagged behind us. I somehow managed to distance myself from Mum and strode into a garage where they sold newspapers, confectionery and drinks. By the time she caught up with me I had helped myself to a drink from the chill cabinet and was heading out of the door without making any attempt to pay for it or even to acknowledge the attendant who was trying to gain my attention. Mum blocked my exit and hurriedly explained that I was not a common thief. She had no money on her so she left her name, address and telephone number and promised to return shortly with the correct payment. She also left her watch because she needed to take another drink for my brother as she knew I wouldn't share. I will now, but usually only if I am asked to do so.

I have improved considerably over the years but if asked why, my parents would be unable to answer. We have tried many therapies and treatments, most of which have been expensive but you could never see anything immediately. They don't work like an operation where you go in with a broken leg and someone fixes it. With autism most of the treatments and therapies work over a long period of time and what works for one will not necessarily be beneficial to another. You just have to try whatever you feel might be appropriate. I cannot recommend or dismiss any of the different therapies. I might have got to this point in my development without any intervention at all but I will never know. Currently I am having homeopathic treatment with Julian to work on my use of words for conversation rather than just to get what I want or need and it seems to be having a positive effect. At least I know to say 'hello' now. Mum wishes she had met Julian twelve years ago because apparently there is a homeopathic version of the MMR vaccine available. Although there have been no trials as yet to prove it works, it has to make sense for those children for whom injections are not advisable.

We only visit close friends and family because I am not particularly good at understanding why you can do things in some places and not others. Why can't I just wander round rooms and look inside cupboards? If I'm hungry and thirsty, what is wrong with just helping myself to something from the fridge? Why can't I check out everyone's video collection and what was the big deal about me walking straight into my old house, putting a video in the machine and sitting on their settee to watch it? I took my shoes off first. (My mum was a bit embarrassed about that, as she didn't know the new owners who had bought the house whilst we were on our short trip abroad. It was also the day of Princess Diana's funeral so they could well have been taping some of the ceremonies. Fortunately, they weren't and were very understanding.) We rarely go anywhere near the house now – just in case!

I am not quite so bad to take shopping these days but if my parents want to 'just look' at things they try to do so on a day when I am not with them. In furniture showrooms I tend to try out all the beds and chairs and they really shouldn't display toilets if they don't want you to use them. Food shopping is okay as I am given the job of trolley pusher. If the aisle is free I usually ride it like a scooter. Daryl hates that. My mum always has her cheque cards on her if she takes me shopping as inevitably at the checkout she'll find more items than she'd actually put in the trolley herself. I'm good at slipping things in whilst her back is turned. It is much quicker these days than it used to be though because I hate labels. I remove them from everything so before barcodes came into operation no one knew what anything cost. This thing about labels also affects all my clothing. It would be no good buying me designer label goods as I'd soon take the scissors to them. My school clothes are all marked with indelible ink.

One thing regularly talked about with autism and indeed many other illnesses is diet and I am on a gluten and casein free diet – sort of. I never ate a variety of food anyway but what I did eat I ate lots of. Unfortunately, it was always the wrong things – chips, crisps, Hula Hoops, crumpets, peperami sausages, batter from fish fingers, pasta, toast, plain biscuits, cereal, milk chocolate and Polo mints. I never ate fruit and vegetables but would consume Oxo and Bovril cubes as if they were sweets. I drank soya sauce from the bottle. I never had hot drinks and would only have milk in shakes. I loved fizzy drinks, coke, lemonade and flavoured squashes and never drank plain water. Amazingly, I was a very healthy child with a beautiful complexion and was very fit and active.

There is a popular belief that certain foods can be harmful to autists because many of them have leaky guts. The reason put forward for this in many cases is the amount of antibiotics they probably had when they were younger. I had lots of antibiotics for ear infections so my parents were concerned that my gut was like a colander and decided to check it out. They contacted a doctor at the Paediatric Research Institute in Norway to see if he could determine whether I was intolerant to anything. Mum sent off urine samples from both my brother and me. It had to be collected over a twenty-four-hour period so she labelled two large plastic beakers D and J and left them in the bathroom. We were supposed to pee in them just a little bit every time we went to the toilet. This was no problem but I noticed that Daryl's was fuller than mine so I tipped some of his into my beaker. Needless to say we had to start all over again.

The results which came back basically said that Daryl was okay but I showed an intolerance to gluten (found in wheat) and casein (found in milk) so my diet was changed. It is incredibly hard though because, apart from the fact that gluten and casein free products are very expensive, they taste awful. The bread is just like pieces of polystyrene. Another problem is that you can't do it half-heartedly because the smallest of small crumbs could affect the result. As it often takes several months to clear your body it becomes a bit of an obsession. You should have separate toasters for normal bread and gluten free bread and if you are on a gluten free diet you can't even make pastry with normal flour in case the gluten gets into your bloodstream through your skin. It's difficult, but we made some adjustments and I have to admit that over a period of time my temperament improved, my concentration span increased and I became much more sociable. Mum even began to question her previous denials that I had been hyperactive. She had always said I was just permanently 'active' but as I was always eating the same things I was most likely permanently 'high'.

At the same time as I started my diet, March 1999, there was a lot of publicity concerning secretin. Someone in America had discovered quite by accident that when her son had been given secretin for something completely unrelated to his autism he had been virtually 'cured'. The interest was phenomenal. Secretin is a polypeptide hormone which basically neutralizes the acids from the stomach as they pass into the small intestine. This allows the pancreatic enzymes to break down food such as protein and fats and if these enzymes don't have the correct pH value they can't work effectively. In autists the proteins from wheat (gluten) and cows' milk (casein) are particularly difficult to break down and there is a risk that if they get absorbed through the leaky gut into the bloodstream they could reach the brain tissue and cause damage. It is called the Opiod Excess Theory.

My parents had me on a gluten and casein free diet but decided they would also like to try the secretin.

However, there was only one doctor in the UK who would administer it via injection and the cost was phenomenal. The reason for this was that, although secretin was registered over here, it was not registered for the purpose of treating autism and therefore the doctor who administered it incurred incredible insurance premiums. (I believe it is cheaper now though – just over £100 per injection – and it is recommended that you have at least four.) A search of the internet by some friends found a place in America where you could get homeopathic secretin in the form of drops. We tried it as apparently the results should be the same as the injection but would take longer. I still take homeopathic secretin but in the form of tablets which come from the UK. I don't know if it is really helping me but I am not the child you read about at the beginning of this story so my parents are loath to stop it.

Of course my self-imposed diet leads to deficiencies. Each day apart from the secretin, I have two capsules containing twenty-two different vitamins and minerals, three calcium and magnesium tablets and two Omega 3 fish oil capsules which are supposed to be beneficial for the brain. No, I don't rattle when I walk.

There have been times in my life when I've shown incredible powers of observation and intelligence. In our kitchen we have five Chinese good luck symbols which my parents bought in Hong Kong. They are displayed on the wall and apparently should be positioned in a certain way or they do not work properly. They are made of brass, all look fairly similar and the only way my parents know what they mean is by turning them over and reading the word on the back. My parents thought they knew the positioning pattern but one weekend when I was in respite care my godmother, who happens to be Chinese, came to stay. She noted that two of the symbols were in the wrong position and changed them round. When I came home the next day the first thing I did when I went into the kitchen was change them back again.

When I was about six or seven years old we were on holiday in a caravan and I wanted to go swimming. Now, as you know, I love water but hate having wet clothes so didn't want to put on my swimming trunks which were still damp from the previous session. To my parents' amazement I simply took out Mum's hairdryer and dried them.

Another time when I was about nine, Mum was going through one of her 'restrict the videos' phases. She thought that if I was unable to sit and watch a film I would surely do something else. Anyway, one summer day whilst I was at school she locked the door to the room where they were all kept and hid the keys, including the spare one. When I came home I walked directly from the taxi straight into the house via the front door. As soon as I realized the video room was locked I looked for the key and when I couldn't find it I asked my mother for it. 'Key please,' I said. She feigned surprise that the door was locked, told me the key had 'gone' and pretended to look for it. Meanwhile I had tried all the other keys we possessed to see if one of them might fit, but of course they didn't. Mum went back to preparing the evening meal and was suddenly aware that a video was playing. She checked to see where it was coming from and when she peered through the keyhole was amazed to see me sitting inside the still-locked room. How did I do it? Well, I went into the lounge and removed the key to the double-glazed (toughened glass) fanlight window which I then used to open the big side window. I climbed out of the lounge and took the key with me. During the walk from the taxi I must have noticed that the fanlight window in the locked room was also open so I climbed up onto the outside window ledge (remember my good sense of balance), leant in and used the key to unlock the big window so I could climb through into the room. Beat that!

I also have a good sense of direction and if you take me somewhere once I can find my way back again.

When we travel along the motorways I always know which turn-off to take. We went to Tenerife when I was about seven years old and the holiday complex we were staying in had two swimming pools. The one we always used was close to our apartment, could be seen from our balcony and was child friendly. It also got the sun for longer than the other one. Once though we had walked all round the complex to see what was available and had looked at the other pool. It was high up on the roof and to get to it you either had to take several steps or go through the main reception area and use the lift.

About a week into our holiday I disappeared. My parents aren't quite sure how I managed to get out of the apartment but I had my trunks on so they guessed I would head for the swimming pool. When they got there I was nowhere to be seen and of course they panicked. I had, after all, no sense of danger and couldn't speak English let alone Spanish. They split up and searched the complex. My dad ran as fast as he could and caught sight of me getting into the lift. By the time I reached the top floor he was there waiting for me, exhausted but happy.

After that we often visited the swimming pool on the top floor where there was a lovely view and a very steep drop to the ground below. I enjoyed that holiday as I didn't stand out. If I spoke in my own special nonsensical language everyone just assumed I was 'foreign'.

Maybe they won't spot me behind these glasses

I have several cousins, two of whom are brothers about the same age as Daryl and me. They argue constantly and drive their parents crazy. My mum is so jealous. She wishes I would fight with Daryl. We get on well but don't really do anything together. Friends of ours who have three boys, the youngest of whom is autistic, feel really sorry for Daryl. They say he is like an only child with none of the advantages.

In their family the two 'normal' boys interact as growing children do and share the responsibility for their autistic younger sibling. In our family there is just Daryl and although he loves me and cares for me deeply my parents worry that when they die I may become a burden for him. It is no use worrying about the future but it is a thought and they have worded their wills accordingly.

I look normal and my autism is invisible. However, I am not, but it is surprising how many people, when they realize I have a problem, ignore me completely or talk about me as though I am not there. It is incredibly rude. Over the years my mother has become stronger and if someone comments about me within earshot she says 'My son is autistic, what's your problem?' This usually works.

It wasn't always so. One hot, sunny Sunday morning my mother took my brother and me to a car boot sale looking for that special toy which would encourage me to play. My grandmother was with us and at some stage bought my brother an ice cream. I never actually ate ice creams – just waved them in front of my eyes like a rocket until they melted, but I made a fuss so my mother decided I wanted one too. My brother didn't come with us to the ice-cream van which was probably just as well. He remained with my gran as I was led off to join the long queue of people waiting patiently in line for the treat of their choice.

Suddenly I arrived and peace was shattered. I did not understand queuing at all so naturally pushed my way to the front. My mother carried me back, explaining as best she could that it was not the done thing. As soon as she released her grip on me I went back to the front. This farce carried on for quite some time with much grumbling from the queue, particularly from mothers with young children. This was perfectly understandable as I looked normal but appeared to be a child with absolutely no manners. I was not setting a good example to their offspring.

Eventually some kind older gentleman obviously twigged that there was more to this situation than met the eye and allowed us to go in front of him in the queue, much to the annoyance of those behind. They were even more annoyed when I finally had to decide what I wanted because I couldn't choose. I didn't know how to say what I wanted. I didn't point and I didn't look at any specific picture so it was very much guesswork. The ice-cream vendor kept thrusting different varieties in my face and I kept knocking them away with a sweep of my hand as if swatting a fly. (It was no good my mother trying to choose for me because if she selected the wrong thing I would have repeated the whole queuing fiasco, which could have been very traumatic and expensive.) In desperation I clambered into the van and helped myself. I'm not sure whether the vendor was surprised or relieved but I got something I could use as a rocket until it dripped down my arm and got discarded. I didn't want to eat it anyway. Trying times.

Another situation which my parents found pretty traumatic was trying to get me to have my photograph taken. My mother had won a family-portrait-sitting competition and decided that as our family were all to be together when the voucher was valid we would have one done. My parents dressed up in their finest. My brother was cool and casual and I wore the clothes I felt comfortable in. Now it is difficult at the best of times to get a good group photograph as there is always one person who is looking the wrong way, blinking or has a peculiar expression on their face at the crucial moment. Our portrait was made even more difficult because I would neither sit still nor look at the camera – at least not when instructed to do so. The photographer was ingenious though because he positioned my parents and brother all smiling beautifully and took a photograph of them. He then took a lovely natural photo of me when I was least expecting it and superimposed my picture on top of the group sitting. Luckily he chose one where I didn't have my finger stuck up my nose. That portrait is much admired in our house, but not as much as the photographer. Oh, the wonders of technology.

Didn't I pose well?

Actually I am quite photogenic and am told I have a lovely smile. I often smile to myself and giggle for seemingly no reason. My brother finds this embarrassing but I am sure you have all done it in your time. How often have you thought of something that has happened in the past and had a little smirk cross your face or even laughed out loud? The only difference between you and me as I see it is that you could, if asked, explain what was making you so happy. I can't, but does that make me crazy?

When children develop they normally go through various stages in a set order. Each stage can be seen as a building block to make a solid individual and it is usual to start with the foundations. If any of these building blocks are missing then the structure can be pretty shaky. Much of my foundation is missing.

Play is a very important building block. It encourages both physical and eye contact, interaction, language and all sorts of other social skills. It is something you just expect every child to do naturally. I never did. I had to be taught how to play and even now I am not very good at it. I am fine with rough and tumble, ball and chasing games as long as they are on my terms and I initiate and end them, but toys and board games hold no interest for me.

Our house is full of toys mostly bought at car boot sales or charity shops. My mother sees no point in spending a lot of money on something I will most likely only ever look at. However, she is the eternal optimist and lives in hope that one day I might just surprise her. Many of the games are suitable for children aged three years upwards. At the moment we are working on a fish game. It consists of several coloured fish all cut up into numbered pieces and a dice. The idea is that players take turns to roll the dice and, depending on the number shown on the upward face, you choose a fish part. The person who completes his or her fish first wins.

I am not competitive and have no problem with coming last every time. I don't care, but I do like to see all the fish in their completed state – neatly lined up in rows and organized. When it is my turn to roll the dice therefore, if the number I throw relates to a part my fish needs I will select it. If another player could use that part I will give it to him or her and if the number is no use to anyone I will just turn the dice around until I find a suitable number to help someone out. It saves so much time. Isn't that being helpful and getting on with people – no jealousy, no envy, no rage?

As I get older some of the things which were so problematic have diminished or disappeared alto-gether, only to be replaced by others. It's all part of growing up I suppose. I still require constant attention as I have difficulty in transferring the knowledge I have to different situations. I am also quite independ-ent in many ways and if I want something done and there is no helpful adult around I will just get on with it with no thought to the possible dangers.

If I am hungry I often try to cook myself pasta or noodles and my mum cringes when she sees me with the boiling water. I love peperami sausages, but only if they are very thinly sliced and fried in their own fat. Generally I go for the sharpest knife in the house and have the frying pan at the ready on a naked gas flame. Sometimes if the electric igniter hasn't worked the frying pan will be on an unlit gas ring. You won't be surprised to hear that smoking is banned in our house.

It's obviously self-service in this kitchen

I also find the microwave very useful but nearly burnt the house down when I programmed it for ten minutes instead of ten seconds. That time we got away with a cracked plate and lots of black smoke everywhere. I am also known for getting the screwdriver and dismantling the video machine if a tape gets stuck inside. That's very good as long as I remember to switch off the electricity supply first.

My helpfulness is not confined to indoors either. I love to wash the car. I have to be carefully supervised with this though because I have a habit of dropping the car sponge on the floor and then picking it straight up complete with small stones to continue my task. Most serious car owners polish their cars after they have been washed – my parents use T-cut. They certainly needed it the day I decided the bonnet would make an ideal slide for my skate board. Wheeee!

OK dad – you just stand there. I'll do the hard work...

I like to paint and am not too messy. I am also fond of DIY. I always use real tools though. Once my dad spent ages cutting a piece of expensive wood to the exact size. He turned his back for a moment and found I had shortened it. I have been known to take the saw to tree branches and when I get out the secateurs our plants really get a good pruning. It's best not to leave matches lying around either as I have inherited my dad's fascination with fires. Yes, the supervision thing is ongoing.

The best thing my parents ever did for me was to accept that I am autistic. They help me as much as they can and expect as much from me as they do from Daryl. They show me how to do things, sometimes hundreds of times, and just occasionally some of it makes sense. We are currently working on self-help skills and I make my own bed, which basically means I pull up the duvet cover in the mornings. I also wash up and dry the dishes but I notice that most of the items I am entrusted with are plastic, unbreakable and not very sharp.

I fold up pants and put socks in pairs once they have been washed and my mum has allowed me to iron some teatowels with help. She is trying to introduce the toilet brush to me but I am resisting that one as long as I can. I understand that some men have managed this for over seventy years so I've got a long way to go yet.

I am being taught to shave and use an electric razor. My mum is a bit concerned because she knows I have seen her shave her legs and under her arms and she is wondering how long it will be before I do the same. Is it just a matter of time? Yes, my growing up is causing her a few headaches. I've discovered that putting my hands down my trousers can be quite a nice experience and Mum's now agonizing over how she's going to impress upon me that there is a time and a place for everything. Think about it.

My parents have tried to really understand why I do the things I do and by getting to know me as well as possible they are sometimes able to alleviate problems before they arise. It causes much less stress all round.

I am shortly to have a tooth out under general anaesthetic. It is an extra one so needs to be removed. I am having it done in hospital and have been told I cannot eat or drink anything after 6.30 am. I usually get up at around 7.00 am and the first thing I do is have something to drink. I then have a shower, get dressed and have my breakfast. I get my own drinks and, as I've already told you, I am quite able to get myself some food if no one else does. My appointment is at 8.30 am which would not be too much of a problem if that was the time of the actual operation. My mum thought she could just whisk me out of the house when I woke up and drive around until it was time to get to the hospital.

However, everyone booked for an operation that day has to arrive at the same time so the nurse and anaesthetist can weigh them, take their blood pressure and decide in which order they will be seen, so theoretically I could be waiting around for hours. The problem then is that I know there is a machine at the hospital which sells drinks and confectionery and if I put some money in I can get what I want. Now you might say that my mum should just not give me any money so I couldn't be tempted. I have come a long way, but not that far. I am big, I am strong and quite capable of causing a scene if I don't get what I want – especially if the reason I can't have it is because I'm having a tooth out. That's not much compensation is it? Which would you rather have – food and drink or an operation? As my dad will not be around for moral and physical support, my mother is planning, so I hear, to visit the clinic before the date of my operation to personally see the surgeon and everyone else involved, explain the situation and see if we can come to some arrangement: that is, having me go in later, be weighed, etc. and then have the tooth removed immediately. It may mean that I will get an early morning view of all the local villages but my mother thinks it is better than what might be the alternative.

There are many things about me that remain a mystery to my parents. They query why I always smell my food. Why will I only eat parts of chips? Why will I only ever eat hard, dry things and not try a more varied diet? Is it the smell, the taste or the texture that determines what I eat? Why am I terrified of cats and dogs and yet have no fear in approaching camels, bulls and highland cattle? Why do I always put labels and stickers on me upside down? Actually that's an easy one – it is so when I look down I can see what they say.

Also, why do I always rub my face against my mother's hair? (Answers on a postcard, please.) Someone recently told my mother that as we develop we let go of certain things in our bodies. I shall call them restrictions because I don't really understand it yet. Anyway, it seems that autists hang on to some of these restrictions and it has been found that if the face is brushed very gently in certain areas around the cheeks and nose it can help. It's a bit like reflexology. The suggestion was therefore made to my mother that I could be trying to get rid of these restrictions myself by using her hair which is soft and gentle. It's yet another theory but I have no doubt that pretty soon the paintbrushes will come out.

I am complex but that's what makes me who I am. I am autistic but I am not stupid. My brain is full of information but sometimes I have difficulty processing it. Someone once explained the autist's brain as being like a huge storage warehouse with no inventory. This seems like a good comparison. Can you imagine the problems Pickford's would have if they didn't know whose box belonged to whom?

I don't know what the future holds for me. The possibilities are endless and we take one day at a time. All I know for certain is that I am making progress and slowly building up my own inventory. I'll get there.

I am on a journey – Jodi's journey.

Another photo of the wild life for the family album

Final word from Mum

I hope you enjoyed *Jodi's Journey* and perhaps now have a slightly better understanding of autism. It is all true but close family members have criticized me for not accurately revealing just how difficult, problematic and painful it has been for us all. I have tried to make the story as humorous as possible but in reality there is nothing funny about autism. It is invisible but demanding. When autism struck my beautiful little boy it ruined his life and the ripple effects spread throughout our family. Fortunately, we are strong, but many families break under the strain. It is hard to fight something you cannot see but you must never give up hope. Jodi is a fine-looking youth and I am sure he will make a handsome man. We accept him as he is but society is less tolerant of adults with strange behaviours than they are of cute little children. We worry for his future and what will become of him.

As I said before there is *nothing* funny about autism.

April 2002